ABSOLU

EFFORTLESS

PROSPERITY

BOOK I

Thirty
Simple Yet Profound Lessons
That Will Transform Your Life
In Thirty Days

2002 REVISED EDITION

Published by
REAL PEOPLE PUBLISHING GROUP
6655 West Sahara Avenue, Suite B200
Las Vegas, Nevada 89146-2832
(702) 222-4014   Fax (702) 222-1644

This book is available at quantity discounts for bulk purchase.
visit www.effortlessprosperity.com

Printed in the United States of America
Real People Publishing Group
Las Vegas, Nevada

ISBN 1-930455-55-0

ISBN 1-930455-55-0

MY PRAYER TO YOU

May every person on earth enjoy a life
of Effortless Prosperity,
living in perfect health, loving relationships,
financial independence, wealth and freedom.

May everyone everywhere realize
a spiritual conscious awakening,
living our lives in love, joy and
Effortless Prosperity.

And so it is.

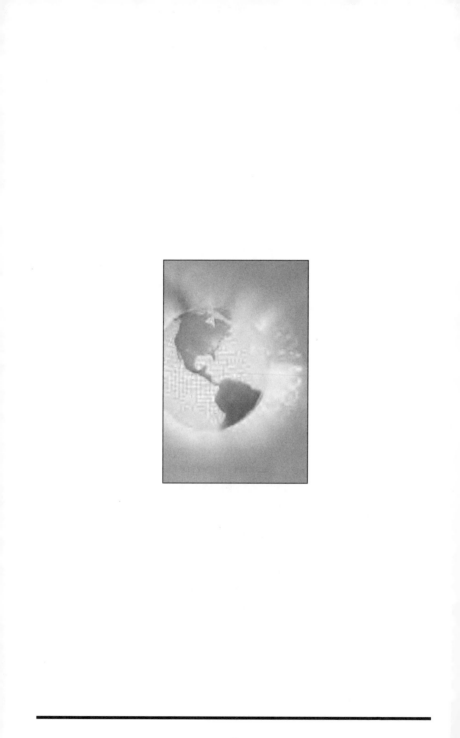

I dedicate this book
to my mother

who was as wonderful in the physical life
as she is now.

Her ability to teach me and guide me
is as profound and as effective today
as it was before her transition
into the spirit world.

Her communications still help and guide me to feel
peace and tranquillity in my life.

I would like to acknowledge
these wonderful earth angels—

my soul mate Samia,
who supports me every moment
with her gentle, loving way;

my son Michael,
who brings me so much love and joy
with his kisses and hugs;

John and Michelle Humphrey,
who are helping to fulfill our dream of spreading the
message of World Peace to the Planet.
Their energy, vision, passion, and support have enabled
more people on the planet the opportunity to create the life
of their dreams;

Bob Coughlan,
for his open heart and support
in getting this vision started;

Donna Visco,
for her great smile, support, and
beautiful artwork and design;

Gary Kadi,
for his love, support, and guidance
in offering his services in coaching and contributing to our
business;

Harriet Tunis,
for the original fine-tuning of this book;

Susan Kallen,
for her great job on original editing,
layout and design—
she expressed my feelings in words
better than anyone I know;

Joel Remde and Janis "Eagle Eye" Cox,
for the editing of the original book;

Kate Haber,
for her amazing flexibility and contribution
in producing the original final edit;

Michael's mom, Kathy;
not only have we healed all past pain between us,
but I am also pleased to have her working with us
as our great webmaster;

My brother John and my sister Terry,
for their unconditional love;

Bill Ganz, Daren Ulmer, and the staff of Corporate
Production Design for their expertise and creativity, in
producing and filming
of the products and infomercial.

Susan Davlin and the entire
Real People Publishing Group team
for their expertise and dedication to quality.

Last but not least, I would like to acknowledge all my
beautiful guides and angels.
I Love You All!

CONTENTS

Always remember Bijan's Law:

*Everything that CAN
go right
WILL go right.*

EXPECT MIRACLES!

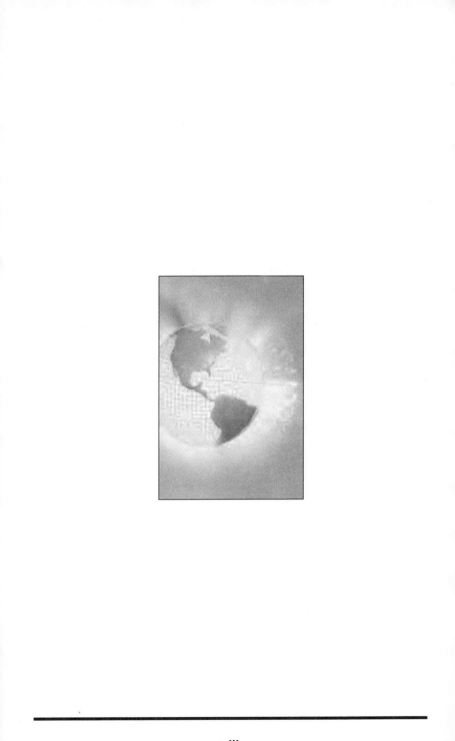

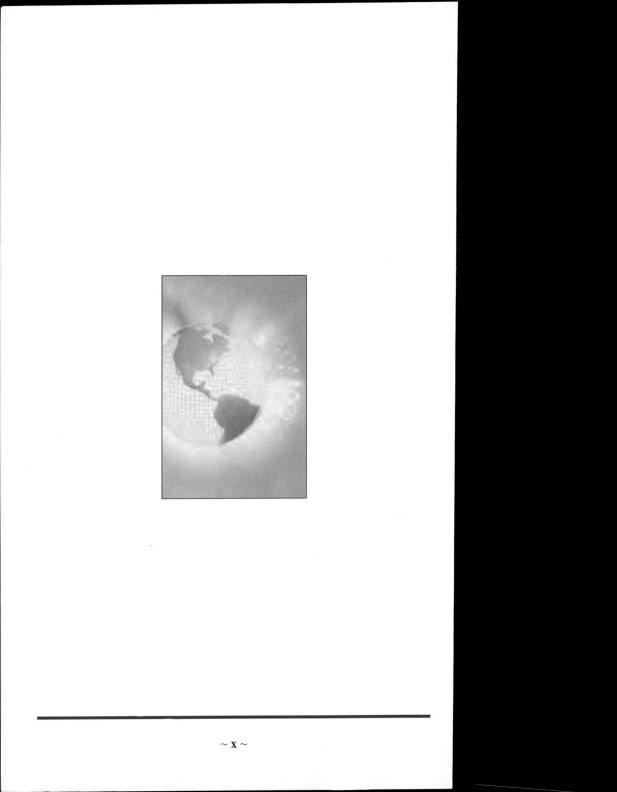

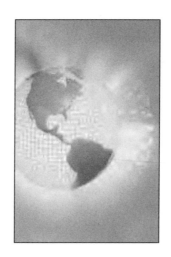

INTRODUCTION

Prosperity
is the ability to be open to receive
all the gifts God has to offer.

It is the ability to know
that enjoying all the gifts God has to offer
is our natural state of being;
it is our inheritance.

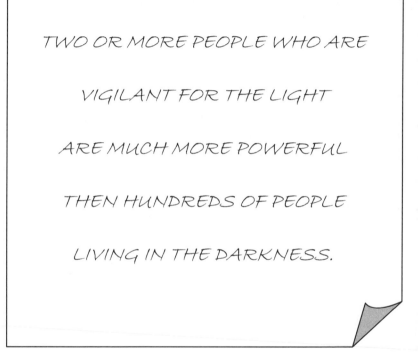

TWO OR MORE PEOPLE WHO ARE

VIGILANT FOR THE LIGHT

ARE MUCH MORE POWERFUL

THEN HUNDREDS OF PEOPLE

LIVING IN THE DARKNESS.

HOW IT ALL BEGAN

In the summer of 1995, after a weekly seminar session on *A Course in Miracles*, several people approached me to say how much they appreciated my sharing. They told me that listening to *my* miracles always helped them to make changes in *their* lives, and they suggested that I write a book about my miracles. I promised I would think about it, and added that I would ask my guide how he felt.

After my meditation the next morning, I discussed the idea with my guide. He told me that I was going to write a book…but not yet. "Now would be a good time," I responded, "since I am not very busy and it is fresh in my mind…."

Again he said, "Not yet."

I let the matter go. Around November, though, while in the middle of an intense workout in preparation for the Mr. Universe competition, my guide suddenly announced, "Bijan. It is time."

"Time? Time for what?" I asked.

He said, "It is time for you to begin writing the book." I told him that I did not know what to write. "Don't worry," he said. "I will handle it. I will tell you what to say and you will write it down."

I began giving him a long list of reasons why this was not a good time for me to begin. "This would be the *worst* time," I insisted. "The real estate market is so busy and I am involved in several large transactions. Also, my diet requires a great deal of attention as I'm getting ready for this competition, and at this particular moment, I am involved in an intensive workout. I don't really have any *time* to write a book."

He listened to all my reasons and said, "Bijan, I told you, it is time. Just do it."

Still, I had even more excuses for him. "…and as you know," I said, "I do not like to write, and I do not like to read; I like to listen. My vocabulary, spelling, and grammar are not that good, either…so it's going to be *very* effortful."

He listened patiently, and then said, "I'll handle it."
Though I was still skeptical, I agreed to write the book, and then I simply let it go.

That same afternoon when I went to my son's school to pick him up I ran into a friend who used to attend *A Course in Miracles* class that I taught on Monday nights. When she asked me how things were going, I smiled and told her what my guide had said. "This is perfect timing," she told me. "My ex-husband does not usually see our children very often, so I am normally very busy taking care of them, but he just informed me that he would like to have them two days a week. I have written books before, and I am very good on the computer," she announced. "I would love to help you type your book." Suddenly I realized what my guide had meant when he said that it was going to be effortless.

I drove to her home two days a week for several months. We would meditate, she would fix me a wonderful cup of tea, and then she would type my miracles as I dictated them to her. Our thinking was in total alignment; this was necessary for me in order to convey the message of the book. The level of mutual understanding, especially of my miracles, felt comfortable, natural and—most importantly—very effortless. Sometimes it seemed as if she knew what I was going to say even before I said it. Finally we felt that our work together was complete. I have a deep love for this friend, and I am very grateful for her contribution.

When the book was finished, I found a printer I could easily work with, and after some discussion we decided to print five thousand copies. But then, during my meditation the following morning, my guide told me to print only one hundred. This troubled me, since it would be far more expensive to publish one hundred than five thousand. My guide assured me that I should do it this way because I might wish to add to the book.

Not too long afterward, I found out he was right. During one of my morning meditations, when I was enjoying an especially abundant feeling of thankfulness and gratitude for my prosperity, my guide appeared with a message. He said that in order for me to be truly prosperous, I must *share* what I have.

Immediately, I asked, "Who do I give it to, and how much?"

With a patient smile, he said, "Bijan, in order for a person to be truly prosperous, he must share his *prosperity consciousness* with others."

I did not completely understand his statement, and sat in quiet puzzlement. Noticing this, he continued by informing me that I was to hold group meetings in which many people could learn about effortless living. I was to select fifty people to participate in the first thirty-day *Effortless Prosperity* seminar, where everyone could share their miracles and results.

I reminded him that my English was not perfect and my vocabulary was limited. He told me that he would take care of it.

"How?" I asked him.

"When you are addressing the people who come to your seminars," he replied, "just get yourself—your

Ego—out of the way, and *I* will speak through you in such a way that those who are *open* to hear the message I am sharing, will *receive* it." A warm feeling filled my heart as I realized that, with the help of my guide, I was going to be able to do this.

Over two hundred seventy people signed up for the *Effortless Prosperity* seminar, and I selected fifty of them to participate. At the end of the thirty days I was guided and directed to specific people and places that would play a part in my offering additional seminars. Within a short time, there was an Effortless Prosperity Center with seminars every two hours from 6 A.M. to 8 P.M., seven days a week. It seemed that everyone I approached was gladly accommodating me and supporting me on my path.

The most extraordinary part of all this was that I never had to *do* anything to prepare what I was going to speak about at the seminars. Instead, I simply had to show up at the designated time and my guide would provide all that was required. To this day, whenever I think about an upcoming seminar, my Ego panics because it thinks that I must prepare myself—but then I always hear the reassuring voice of my guide telling me, "YOU NEED DO NOTHING."

Now I offer this book to you in hope that, by the sharing of my Effortless Prosperity consciousness with you, you will also experience the miracles that will guide you in changing your life—effortlessly.

As your perception shifts, you will see your world differently; you will come to realize how powerful you are, and that you are the creator of your own Universe.

As you begin the thirty days of lessons, it is important to understand and remember two important truths:

- This book is not about *doing* things; doing is in the realm of effect and the body—where Ego creates fear and limitation. Instead, this book is about *being*, which is in the realm of cause and the mind—where free will and choice are always possible.

- The results that you experience will be equal to the commitment you make in following your daily lessons.

I love you—
My blessing is with you always!

Bijan

HOW TO BE
EFFORTLESSLY PROSPEROUS

To be prosperous without effort, we must first decide to make peace our ultimate goal. To be in peace, we must know that our *only* function in life is to heal ourselves and others through our expressions of love and forgiveness.

To be prosperous without effort, we do not have to get better jobs or second jobs, or to work more hours. We do not have to add to our education, acquire additional degrees, or make better contacts. We do not have to be around people who either lead us or follow us, or are more successful than we are. We have only to stay focused on our function of *healing* and our goal of *peace* as we participate in life through interaction with people in our personal relationships, jobs and social activities.

One of the greatest benefits of following the guidelines of *Absolutely Effortless Prosperity* is that we become aware of how we project our own feelings of guilt and fear onto others. It is Ego that will always tell us we are guilty or afraid, and that we do not deserve effortless prosperity. At the same time, Ego will convince us that we must get rid of our guilt—and will tell us to do this by projecting it onto others. Once we understand what Ego has us doing, we realize that everyone is simply our mirror. In other words, what we see in other people is actually what is inside ourselves. As we learn to *see* this as *our own* guilt being projected out to other people, we are able to forgive them; by loving and forgiving them, we are loving and forgiving ourselves and can heal our own minds.

Every experience in life is an opportunity for us to do our function of healing. Though healing may seem difficult at times, it is made easier when we practice and think about it as often as possible. The thirty easy, yet powerful lessons of this book, when practiced, allow Ego to be slowly pushed out of the way so that Holy Spirit is allowed to enter. This provides us with all that we require to experience effortless prosperity. Also, these lessons have been designed to give us the vision to see that, through our Ego-selves, we can do nothing—but with the help of Holy Spirit, our Higher Self and our guides, we can achieve our ultimate goal of peace simply by performing our daily function of healing ourselves and others.

As we perform our function of healing, our lives will become peaceful and effortless. Everything around us will automatically fall into place and everything that we require will be provided for us. God knows what we desire, even before we ask; as long as we are vigilant for the light and we always choose peace, our lives will be filled with effortless prosperity, effortless relationships, effortless health, and—ultimately—effortless living.

HOW TO USE THIS BOOK

Absolutely Effortless Prosperity Book I is a guide into the realm of Truth—where we are divinely provided with everything we desire to be totally prosperous. It has been created to produce maximum results in the shortest time possible.

Absolutely Effortless Prosperity Book I is not a book to be read in one sitting—the total power and effectiveness of this course comes from the daily reading of and vigilance for the lesson of the day. One by one, day by day, each lesson builds upon the next to create effortless prosperity consciousness.

If you sincerely "live" the lessons one hundred percent each day, sharing your miracles with everyone else or with an *Effortless Prosperity* group, you will experience what it is to be effortlessly prosperous by the end of thirty days. If you are not vigilant, and are only partially committed to living the lessons, you may have to practice them for more than one thirty-day period.

It may take only a month to get it, or it may take six months or more, but each additional month you follow the thirty lessons of *Absolutely Effortless Prosperity*, you will experience them on a different level.

The following are five suggestions that will ensure the best results:

- *Begin with the lesson that corresponds to the day of the month.* For example, if you start on the 11th day of the month, read all of the lessons up to and including Lesson 11. Then, on the next day, read Lesson 12.

- *Sit quietly for several minutes* each morning after rising, and each evening before retiring, while you repeat your lesson for the day. Allow communication and spiritual guidance to come to you during this time. These lessons will put you in touch with knowing the truth of who you are—a child of God.

- *Apply each lesson you have learned,* as often as possible throughout the day. As a reminder, you may wish to write the day's lesson on a piece of paper, or on the palm of your hand. Whenever you think of it during the day, read the lesson to yourself slowly, with full attention, absorbing the words into your being. Since each lesson builds upon and confirms the previous lessons, some participants have found it extremely beneficial to reread each of the previous lessons along with the lesson of the day. As a result of bringing all of the lessons into their consciousness each day, they have experienced even faster growth.

- *Be open to receive miracles,* acknowledge them with joy and gratitude, and write your miracles for each day in the Miracle Journal at the end of the book.

- *Share your miracles with others* on a daily basis. Be patient and vigilant. It is easy to return to old habits and familiar belief systems. After all, we have lived with them for a long time. Change is most effective when it is gentle and gradual. That is why this book is made up of thirty simple, yet profound lessons that will help you to create effortless prosperity in your life.

As you go through the lessons, you may experience some resistance. Ego will often raise three issues:

- *First,* it will tell you that effortless prosperity is too good to be true. It will tell you that nothing is effortless—that financial abundance, perfect relationships and excellent health only come with hard work and long hours.

- *Second,* it will tell you that the miracles you experience are just coincidence. Ego does not wish for you to recognize Spirit and your vigilance for the light.

- *Third,* as Ego begins to lose control, it will panic and may become desperate; on a subconscious level, you might begin to feel that you do not deserve effortless prosperity; you may even experience guilt about the past or fear about the future.

It is important to remember that all of this is just Ego's attempt to distract you from the positive things that are happening to you. Ego will place many obstacles in your way, and all of them can be easily overcome, simply by smiling and saying to Ego, "Thank you for sharing!"

Remind yourself often that you are joyous, prosperous and completely open to receive all of God's gifts. You deserve all that the Universe has to offer, and as you remain steadfast to Truth, and trust God within, you will see amazing results.

HOW TO SHARE MIRACLES

Miracles are shifts in perception. They occur when we ask Spirit to guide us in seeing something through Spirit's eyes rather than Ego's.

Miracles are a natural occurrence; they are expressions of love. When our flow of love is blocked, they do not show up; instead of miracles, we experience turmoil.

Miracles heal the emotions of fear, separation, guilt and anger. They always fill us with peace, because when we share *only* miracles, we are speaking in the language of *light*.

By sharing miracles every day, we encourage ourselves and others to continue looking for and acknowledging them. The more miracles we look for, the more miracles we will find.

It is recommended that you write your miracles in your journal as soon as possible, before you forget them. Given enough time, Ego may work to dispel the miracles and make it difficult for you to remember them when it is time for you to share.

There is an important difference between telling a story and sharing a miracle. Stories include all of the guilt, blame and fear leading up to the miracle, and show the cause as being anywhere else but within ourselves. Ego likes to add to the story because it believes that the longer the story and the deeper the drama, the juicier the miracle will be in the end. However, the truth is that after several minutes of listening to someone share a story, our minds become so filled with the illusion of fear that we do not have enough capacity left to receive the miracle. We can literally feel the peaceful energy drain out of our bodies.

Stories always bring turmoil to both the speaker and the listener. Limiting the shares—which are always confidential—to only two or three minutes will help to ensure against *story* telling.

ABOUT WORLD PEACE

The mass consciousness of this planet Earth has never seen or been aware of true world peace. All of our history dictates war and separation in the pursuit of peace; the belief system on this planet is that peace can only be achieved by force and domination. I believe that unless there is a sense of peace already in the consciousness of *every person on the planet*, world peace will be virtually impossible to achieve.

In truth, world peace can only be achieved from the inside out. As each individual feels joy and peace within, extending it outward to family and friends, and extending it even further to all who are encountered in daily life, slowly the mass consciousness will change from one of fear, force and domination to one of love. Then, and only then, will we have peace on our planet.

Each lesson in *Absolutely Effortless Prosperity* is about bringing joy and peace to you and your surroundings. However, the affirmation at the bottom of each lesson is about more than just you and your surroundings. It is about raising your consciousness and vibration high enough that your light of joy and peace will shine outward, touching others who will then also shine and touch others, as the energy shifts toward realizing peace on Earth.

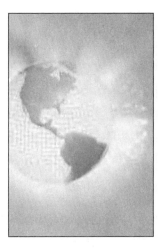

This book is going to help and support you by focusing your thoughts on peace and spirit. You must know that it is a world of belief systems, meaning whatever you think and believe you experience.

By learning how to control your thoughts more and more, through the daily lessons that focus on peace, joy, love, and prosperity, you will soon notice that you will start to think differently about each situation and truly experience a more effortless life.

THE
LESSONS

*You will be
totally peaceful
and effortlessly prosperous
after thirty days
only when you **be** and **live** the lessons
every day, all day;
this is in the realm
of Spirit.*

*When you
read them, study them
and analyze them,
this is in the realm
of Ego.*

DAY 1 ~ LESSON 1

I WATCH WHAT I SAY

Today I am aware of all the things I say. I look at *what* I am saying, how much I am talking, and how much of what I am saying is making a difference in my life. Am I speaking for peace, or am I speaking for turmoil? Am I speaking to bring more joy and love, or am I speaking to bring more fear? Throughout this day, I am aware of what I am saying, and I choose to speak only words of joy, peace and love to myself and others. *Today I watch what I say.*

RECOMMENDED READING
About Ego (p. 53)
Keeping Your Word (p. 55)
You Always Get What You Want (p. 57)

ASSIGNMENT FOR DAY 1
Be aware of how much you keep your word today.

Affirmation: I speak only for peace.
Remember to keep your word today.

I NOTICE WHAT I HEAR

Today I am aware of what really attracts me the most. Am I listening for miracles, peace and love, or am I listening for stories, turmoil and fear? At every moment, I can make a choice of listening to Spirit or to Ego. At every moment, I am aware of which one I am listening to, and I refuse to listen to Ego. *Today I notice what I hear.*

RECOMMENDED READING
I Am Just the Messenger (p. 60)
A Message from "Our Friend" (p. 63)

ASSIGNMENT FOR DAY 2
Be aware of what you are listening to; be aware of whether you enjoy listening to Spirit or to Ego.

Affirmation: I listen only for peace.
Remember to keep your word today.

DAY 3 ~ LESSON 3

I AM AWARE OF WHAT I SEE

Today I am aware of what I am looking at and what I am watching for. Am I more interested in looking at an accident and someone getting a ticket on the freeway, or do I enjoy seeing the sunlight filter through my window? Do I experience more powerful emotions watching someone fight than I do watching a child sleep? Am I interested in all the shooting and violence on the news, or do I notice people holding hands and expressing joy? When I realize that I have a choice of where and upon what I cast my gaze, I will choose to see only positive things. What I see affects my mind, and it is my mind that creates the world outside of me. *Today I am aware of what I see.*

RECOMMENDED READING
Reliving Hurtful Experiences (p. 66)
Choosing Joy or Fear (p. 67)

ASSIGNMENT FOR DAY 3
Give some money away—not because the recipient deserves it. Bless it. Notice how you feel.

Affirmation: I see peace everywhere.
Remember to keep your word today.

DAY 4 ~ LESSON 4

I DO NOT KNOW THE
REAL MEANING OF WHAT I SEE

Everything that I see happening around me has a meaning that I have given to it. When I am willing to let go of thinking that I know the real meaning, I notice that it is much different from what I thought it was. Today I realize and understand that the meaning I give to anything has nothing to do with its real purpose. *I do not know the real meaning of what I see.*

RECOMMENDED READING
I Am Not a Body (p. 68)
Whatever You Resist Will Persist (p. 70)

ASSIGNMENT FOR DAY 4
Do something nice for yourself today. Examples: get a massage; go out for dinner; treat yourself to something that brings you joy and peace.

Affirmation: I am surrounded by peace.
Remember to keep your word today.

DAY 5 ~ LESSON 5

I AM WILLING TO SEE THE LIGHT

Today I am willing to see the light, which is always available to me; I allow it to come in and brighten up my day. I see it even in the darkest situations. By opening my eyes and my mind to the light, I experience joy, love, happiness, prosperity and abundance. I am open for miracles to happen. *I am willing to see the light, every hour of this day.*

RECOMMENDED READING
Recognizing a Savior (p. 71)
Uncovering the Light (p. 75)

ASSIGNMENT FOR DAY 5
Do something special for someone special—
in action, or in a kind word.

Affirmation: I know only peace inside.
Remember to keep your word today.

DAY 6 ~ LESSON 6

I AM VIGILANT FOR THE LIGHT

Today I am more aware of my thoughts, and I choose thoughts of the light rather than of darkness. Regardless of how attractive the thoughts of darkness may look—or how rewarding Ego says they will be— I know the difference between light and dark thoughts. Today, I repeat the words "I am vigilant for the light" to myself as many times as possible. I choose light over darkness and love over fear. *Today I am vigilant for the light, all day long.*

RECOMMENDED READING
Going Home to Peace (p. 76)
The Game of Life (p. 79)

ASSIGNMENT FOR DAY 6
In the morning after reading the lesson, sit quietly and ask yourself whom you resent. The first person who comes to mind is the right person. Make an attempt to contact this person: talk face-to-face, call on the telephone, write, or meditate and clear the resentment.

Affirmation: I am vigilant for peace.
Remember to keep your word today.

I AM VERY PROSPEROUS

Today I understand that I am not my ego or the name I was given at birth. In truth, I am *who I really am*—an extension of God and a very, very prosperous creator. If Ego appears today and tells me I have too little money in the bank, I owe money to people, or my job does not pay me enough, I simply remember that none of this has anything to do with *who I really am*. As an extension of God, I am very prosperous. The moment I believe I am prosperous beyond a shadow of a doubt, everything around me will change to reflect this truth. My abundance is overwhelming and is only waiting to be received by me. *I am very prosperous.*

RECOMMENDED READING
Prosperity (p. 81)
Expanding My Prosperity (p. 87)

ASSIGNMENT FOR DAY 7
When you get up in the morning, see yourself as a ball of light that is very powerful, like the sun. All day, walk around saying "I am the light," and shine upon everyone.

Affirmation: I am so peaceful.
Remember to keep your word today.

EVERYONE WISHES TO CONTRIBUTE TO ME

Today I realize that everyone is making a contribution to my life. Everyone wishes to assist me in creating everything I desire, not because of what I say or do, but because deep inside there is a *knowing* that I am prosperous, and at an even deeper level, there is a *knowing* that we are *all* prosperous. Everyone's joy, happiness and function are to contribute to me; I must only receive and accept this as a natural part of my being. *Everyone wishes to contribute to me.*

RECOMMENDED READING
Weakening the Ego (p. 89)
How Prosperity Works (p. 90)

ASSIGNMENT FOR DAY 8
Give up control with one person or one issue for the day. Look at the result and your reaction to it. The result will be what is best for you.

Affirmation: I see peace in everyone's actions.
Remember to keep your word today.

DAY 9 ~ LESSON 9

I DESERVE PROSPERITY

Today I know that because of who I am—a child of God—I deserve all of God's gifts. They are my inheritance. When I open my mind and heart, I see myself as a very wonderful person who deserves everything that is good. And when I say, "I deserve prosperity," meaning it with my whole heart, I allow prosperity to come forth, to complete and fulfill me. *I deserve prosperity.*

RECOMMENDED READING
Miracles Are Not Sized (p. 91)
A Lesson in Forgiveness (p. 92)

ASSIGNMENT FOR DAY 9
Be dedicated to laugh. The more you laugh, the more that prosperity comes to you. Laugh all day long. If people are with you, make them laugh, too.

Affirmation: My planet Earth deserves peace.
Remember to keep your word today.

DAY 10 ~ LESSON 10

I AM OPEN TO RECEIVE
ALL OF GOD'S GIFTS

Today—all day—I literally walk around with my hands open to receive. I am not surprised when I realize that I am receiving without having to *do* anything. When someone offers to contribute something to me, I accept graciously. Knowing that each gift is a gift from God, I experience profound thankfulness and gratitude within myself; God hears my thankfulness and gratitude, and responds with more gifts from many sources. *Today I remember to keep saying to myself "I am open and receiving all of God's gifts."*

RECOMMENDED READING
Asking for What You Want (p. 94)
Remembering My Source (p. 96)

ASSIGNMENT FOR DAY 10
Walk around all day with your hands open to receive. Imagine your spiritual self walking around with hands open to receive.

Affirmation: I see world peace.
Remember to keep your word today.

DAY 11 ~ LESSON 11

I GIVE AS I RECEIVE

I know that giving and receiving are the same thing. It is just as joyous to give as it is to receive. It is just as joyous to receive as it is to give. When I *give* joyously, *I* am healed by doing my function of making a contribution to another. When I *receive* joyously, the *give*r is healed by doing his or her function of making a contribution to me. *Today I give as I receive.*

RECOMMENDED READING
Forgiving Others to Forgive Myself (p. 98)
Cause and Effect (p. 103)

ASSIGNMENT FOR DAY 11
See at least one person as a child of God. Show this person unconditional love. You will feel honored to be in his or her presence.

Affirmation: I wish peace for everyone.
Remember to keep your word today.

DAY 12 ~ LESSON 12

I RELEASE ALL FEAR

Today I let go of my fear of anything, and I trust God to take the fear away. The way that I let go is simply by *knowing* that fear does not exist. I truly know that fear is simply *Ego's* deluded perception that it is possible to experience a lack of love in my life. To release this deluded perception, I must *know* that I am always filled with, and surrounded by, unconditional love. Whenever I experience fear, I can bring forth this unconditional love, and immediately the fear will disappear. *Today I release all fear.*

RECOMMENDED READING
Honesty (p. 104)
The Beauty of the Present (p. 106)

ASSIGNMENT FOR DAY 12
Write five to ten affirmations of joy and prosperity for yourself. Repeat them throughout the day.

Affirmation: I embrace only peace.
Remember to keep your word today.

DAY 13 ~ LESSON 13

I OPEN MY MIND TO PEACE

Today I open my mind to the realization that there is always another way to view any experience in life. Whenever an experience does not bring me peace, I look at it from a different perspective. By being aware of the possibility that there is another way of looking at the experience, I create the opportunity for a peaceful resolution. *Today I open my mind to peace.*

RECOMMENDED READING
Grateful Surrender (p. 107)
Excitement in the Present (p. 109)

ASSIGNMENT FOR DAY 13
Find a homeless person and give that person some money. When you do, notice your judgment. That judgment is about you.

Affirmation: I open my life to peace.
Remember to keep your word today.

DAY 14 ~ LESSON 14

I RECOGNIZE
MY OWN BEST INTEREST

I am aware that whatever I see is only a small part of the whole picture. Because I cannot *see* the whole picture, usually what I think is good for me is not, and what I think will hurt me is actually helpful. In opening myself to this knowledge, I finally understand that I can let go of taking a chance at being right or wrong, because my own best interest is what is always being served in my life. *Today I give up resistance and recognize my own best interest.*

RECOMMENDED READING
Serving My Own Best Interest (p. 110)
Sharing the Lessons of Others (p. 112)

ASSIGNMENT FOR DAY 14
Hug someone you normally would not hug. This is to be a sincere hug, not a quick one. What goes through your mind and how do you feel about yourself as you hug this person?

Affirmation: Peace is all I desire.
Remember to keep your word today.

DAY 15 ~ LESSON 15

I AM PATIENT

Today I am patient with myself and with everyone else, for I know that time exists only to facilitate healing and growing. I know the difference between patience and procrastination, understanding that patience comes from Spirit's love, while procrastination comes from Ego's fear. Today I move through all of my functions and activities effortlessly, with patience and love. *Today I am patient.*

RECOMMENDED READING
Surrendering Control (p. 115)
Seeing the Truth About Myself
Through Others (p. 117)

ASSIGNMENT FOR DAY 15
Thank someone who truly deserves thanking. Come from your heart. How does it feel?

Affirmation: Peace is forever.
Remember to keep your word today.

DAY 16 ~ LESSON 16

I PAUSE BEFORE I REACT

Because I know that Ego always jumps in first to *react* to occurrences in my life, I remember to pause and allow Spirit's love to come through me, so I may *respond* to any situation. When I respond from Spirit, a result is produced that is good for me and for everyone else. I pause, let go of my initial ego-oriented reaction, clear my mind, and ask for guidance. I receive guidance and act upon it. *Today I pause before I react.*

RECOMMENDED READING
Love or Discipline (p. 119)
Judgment (p. 120)

ASSIGNMENT FOR DAY 16
Beginning with today, start *being* instead of *doing*. Expect a miracle—a *big* miracle.

Affirmation: I love peace.
Remember to keep your word today.

I AM OPEN
TO RECEIVE MIRACLES

Miracles are a natural part of my life, and my acknowledgement of them makes them real for me. Miracles are the expression of unconditional love. They are always available to me; they are my inheritance from God.   *Today I am open to receive miracles.*

RECOMMENDED READING
Traffic Miracles (p. 121)
Remembering My Goal (p. 123)

ASSIGNMENT FOR DAY 17
Treat yourself special. Know that *who you are inside* deserves the best. Feel unconditionally loved. Give yourself anything you desire. Today you are a loving and lovable king or queen.

Affirmation: I see everyone peaceful.
Remember to keep your word today.

DAY 18 ~ LESSON 18

I CHOOSE ONLY PEACE

Today I choose peace over everything else; I choose peace all throughout the day. Every decision I make will be based on this. *No matter what my options are, today I choose only peace.*

RECOMMENDED READING
Gift from a Friend (p. 125)
Having Goals (p. 127)

ASSIGNMENT FOR DAY 18
Spend the day in silence. Speak only if you must, and only to bring light and peace.

Affirmation: I love my peace.
Remember to keep your word today.

I AM LOVING AND LOVABLE

Today I constantly repeat to myself that I am loving
and lovable. I feel loving toward all others, and I am
worthy of their love, as well. I love myself, I love
everyone, and everyone loves me. No matter what
Ego tries to tell me, I know that I am worthy of love.
Today I know that I am loving and lovable.

RECOMMENDED READING
Gifts from the Father (p. 128)
Projecting My Guilt (p. 129)

ASSIGNMENT FOR DAY 19
Continue to stay in peace. Throughout the day,
repeatedly say to yourself, "I am wonderful and kind,
and so worthy and deserving of all God's gifts." Say
"Thank you, God," "I love God," "God loves me,"
and "I love me."

Affirmation: God shines peace on me.
Remember to keep your word today.

DAY 20 ~ LESSON 20

ONLY LOVE EXISTS;
FEAR IS AN ILLUSION

Today I know that only love exists, and fear is an illusion. Fear is a lack of love, just as darkness is a lack of light. To remove the illusion of fear, I simply bring forth love; I then notice that fear has gone and Truth has returned. *Only love exists; fear is an illusion.*

RECOMMENDED READNG
Love Does Not Punish (p. 131)
Seeing Through the Eyes of Love (p. 135)

ASSIGNMENT FOR DAY 20
Tell one person that you love him or her. Be in the present, and have the words come from your heart. Notice the reaction; the person you tell will never forget the moment. Express the love until you connect—until you really feel it. Notice *your* reaction, as well.

Affirmation: Peace is within me.
Remember to keep your word today.

DAY 21 ~ LESSON 21

GOD LOVES ME UNCONDITIONALLY

Today I feel peaceful. I am so comfortable that I have a warm, fuzzy feeling inside. I know that God is taking care of me. The power of the Universe is with me, and it protects me from all harm; it even protects me from my own dark thoughts. As I allow all grievances, anger, fear, turmoil and other negativity to fall away, my perception is changed and I am open to the unconditional love that is always available to me. I am happy and peaceful in knowing that *God loves me unconditionally.*

RECOMMENDED READING
Letting Go of What I Want (p. 137)
The Love of God (p. 139)

ASSIGNMENT FOR DAY 21
Hold someone's hand and, without speaking aloud, let that person know that you love him or her unconditionally.

Affirmation: I feel God's peace now.
Remember to keep your word today.

GOD LOVES ME
MORE THAN I LOVE MYSELF

Today I know that all of my experiences happen for a reason, and I choose to see each experience as part of my function of healing. Because of this, I can give up control and let God lead the way. God knows what is best for me, far better than I do. *Today I know that God loves me more than I love myself.*

RECOMMENDED READING
The Path of Life (p. 140)

ASSIGNMENT FOR DAY 22

Listen for God's voice to guide you today. When you are making a decision, the voice will be clearest and strongest. Be still, and simply listen. God's voice always brings peace; Ego's voice only brings turmoil.

Affirmation: God's peace and mine are one.
Remember to keep your word today.

DAY 23 ~ LESSON 23

I TRUST GOD

Today I am aware that I have not been trusting God completely. When I trust God, I do not question any event that happens, for I know that everything that occurs in my life is in my best interest. My power to create miracles for myself begins as I realize that I can make a conscious choice to trust God. *Today I trust God.*

RECOMMENDED READING
Unfortunate Circumstances—or Gifts? (p. 143)

ASSIGNMENT FOR DAY 23
Listen for God within, and embrace the peace that He offers you. Then notice and acknowledge the experience you have in your life because of it. Can you see the good—the silver lining?

Affirmation: I trust peace.
Remember to keep your word today.

GOD IS GREAT, AND SO AM I

I already know that I am an extension of God. His quality and His essence are within me; they are inherent and are my natural state. I am a child of God, and have the potential to be just like Him. God is great, and so am I. Whenever I must bring love into my perception of another person, I close my eyes, remind myself that we are *all* extensions of God, and repeat the words "God is great, and so are you." *God is great, and so am I.*

RECOMMENDED READING
Healing My Perceptions (p. 144)
Decision-Making in the Present (p. 146)

ASSIGNMENT FOR DAY 24
Acknowledge how wonderful you are. Know that you are magnificent and that you are growing toward the light. Know that many people are growing with you.

Affirmation: Peace is great.
Remember to keep your word today.

DAY 25 ~ LESSON 25

I LET GO AND LET GOD

Today I surrender control, and I allow the part of God that is expressing through me to come into my life to guide me. Today I let peace make all of my decisions; I let love tell me where to go, whom to see, and what to say; I let the part of me that is God shine forth, creating joy in my life. Today I have the trust to surrender control. *I let go and let God.*

RECOMMENDED READING
Looking Beyond Judgment (p. 147)

ASSIGNMENT FOR DAY 25
For one day, give full control to God. Do not take back the control. Surrender to His care and love, all day long. Notice how you feel.

Affirmation: I shine peace.
Remember to keep your word today.

I AM BLESSED
AS A CHILD OF GOD

As a child of God, I have all the gifts of life available to me at every moment. The gifts of joy, peace, love, prosperity, abundance, power and choice are mine; they are already in my life. As I acknowledge and recognize these gifts, they manifest more frequently and abundantly. My blessings are infinite, and my life is filled with peace and absolutely effortless prosperity. *I am blessed as a child of God.*

RECOMMENDED READING
A Problem With Men (p. 150)

ASSIGNMENT FOR DAY 26
Bless people—either silently or aloud—all day long. Say, "God bless you" to everyone, and mean it.

Affirmation: I have the peace of God.
Remember to keep your word today.

TODAY BELONGS TO GOD;
IT IS MY GIFT TO HIM

Today I give and share all that I am. Knowing this day is already taken care of, I give up control and dedicate everything to God. *Today belongs to God; it is my gift to Him.*

RECOMMENDED READING
Our Function (p. 151)

ASSIGNMENT FOR DAY 27
Do not make any decision, small or large, without first asking God, your guides or your angels. If the question comes from your heart, and you are open to receive guidance, you will hear the answer.

Affirmation: I am one with peace.
Remember to keep your word today.

DAY 28 ~ LESSON 28

I SEE ONLY GOD
IN ALL OF MY AFFAIRS

Today I am completely vigilant for the light in everything I do. I know, at every moment, that everything happens to bring me closer to my goal, which is peace. Every action I take comes from my willingness to do my function of healing. *Today I see only God in all of my affairs.*

RECOMMENDED READING
Where We Do God's Work (p. 153)
On the Death of a Loved One (p. 155)

ASSIGNMENT FOR DAY 28
Sit for fifteen minutes in a quiet place—later in the day is preferable. Look at yourself, at your growth. Acknowledge how far you have come.

Affirmation: Peace is everywhere.
Remember to keep your word today.

THANK YOU, GOD

Today I thank God for all that I am. Regardless of what my life looks like at this time, I know that every experience is occurring exactly the way it is supposed to, for my highest good. I give thanks for this, and I continue on to each new experience, knowing that each is better than the one before, because I now have a greater understanding of who I really am. God is now in control of my life, and I am very thankful. *Today I thank God.*

RECOMMENDED READING
Healing (p. 159)
Guided by Spirit (p. 161)

ASSIGNMENT FOR DAY 29
Say "Thank you," either silently or aloud, to all of the people you meet. Say it sincerely—from your heart. See all of the people you meet as God, just as you see yourself as God. Understand that you are not thanking their Egos, but you are thanking who they truly are. You are thanking the God within them.

Affirmation: Thank you, peaceful Earth.
Remember to keep your word today.

I HEAR GOD'S VOICE ALL DAY

Today I open my mind and heart in such a way that I can hear God speak to me and give me direction. I am open and able to receive His guidance. When He speaks to me, holy ideas come to my mind. God also speaks to me through my brothers and sisters when they are sharing their love with me. *I hear God's voice all day.*

RECOMMENDED READING
To Know What You Want,
Look at What You Have (p. 162)

ASSIGNMENT FOR DAY 30
Thank everyone for his or her inner goodness. Do not thank or agree with Ego; thank the part of everyone that is peaceful. Thank everyone's inner being.

Affirmation: I am peace.
Remember to keep your word today.

RECOMMENDED READING

A miracle
is always available.

When you do not experience it,
you are looking
in the wrong place.

ABOUT EGO

When we come to our bodies, we bring forth our Ego, which is a thought of separation based on fear. At that stage, our Ego is like a little puppy which depends only on us. We love it like our own pet, we feed it with our insecurity, we put a leash on it, and we attach the leash permanently to our wrist, like a handcuff.

From that moment on, the more we feed our ego by thinking we are better than others and we are special, or by thinking we are not as good as others and we are guilty, the bigger our ego becomes. Unlike a puppy, our ego's growth is not limited. If we feed it enough, it can grow as big as an elephant, and by that time we will have no control over it whatsoever. In fact, you probably know of certain people with elephant Egos, where the smallest disappointment drives them crazy enough to throw a fit.

If you have ever had a dog, you have noticed that as you take your dog for a walk in the park and someone else is doing the same with a bigger dog, the bigger dog will never attack *you*, but it will attack *your dog*. That is the way Ego is. It only notices or sees other Egos. Spirits are totally unnoticed in this situation.

As long as you listen to your Ego, the thought of separation is fully present and the outcome is always turmoil and entanglement. Our goal is to minimize our ego by not feeding it. This way it will be kept small and weak, and it will not have any choice but to follow us—the spirits that we are. When the Ego follows us, the outcome will be joy, peace and effortless living.

KEEPING YOUR WORD

A dear friend of mine always seemed to be telling me that the Universe was less than kind to him. Even though he made a good amount of money, he always spoke about scarcity. He was never satisfied with anything that happened in his life, and his relationships usually fell apart after a few weeks.

My friend was always complaining to me that the Universe did not ever give him what he asked for. Sometimes he even compared himself to me, asking, "Why do *you* always get what you ask for?"

Every time I heard that question, I would think for a moment and simply reply, "I don't know."

Finally I decided to meditate and consult my guide on this matter. "Why is it that I receive all that I wish for in life and my friend does not?"

My guide answered, "Imagine that God—your Father, your Higher Power—is watching you with shimmering readiness and excitement, waiting to manifest your wishes. When you keep changing your mind and changing your word, saying one thing and then doing another, He gets confused. Not knowing that His son can lie, God watches and listens and then says to Himself, 'My son does not know what he truly desires, but since I am very patient, I will simply wait until he makes up his mind—no matter how long it takes.'"

"Keeping your word is very important for your welfare," my guide continued. "Give your word only when you are positive that you are going to live up to it, and the Universe will come together to provide you with what you ask for. Your friend is very confused; he constantly changes his mind after giving his word. As long as he continues not to keep his word, the Universe will hold back."

"Shall I relay this information to him?" I asked.

"No, not now," my guide said. "I will let you know when to tell him. He is not yet ready for it."

My guide then assured me that we are all growing along the right path. Though we do not have a choice as to the direction of our growth, we do have a choice of how fast we grow or how much we delay it.

YOU ALWAYS GET
WHAT YOU WANT

I had not been on a trip for a while, so I decided to take my eleven-year-old son, Michael, on a short cruise to Mexico. The trip was planned so that we would be on the ship for New Year's Eve, and we were both very excited about the idea of welcoming in the New Year this way.

The morning before the day of our departure, I went to the gym to do my usual workout and ran into an old friend that I had not seen for a while. When I told him how excited I was about the cruise, he suggested that I would have a much better time being by myself and meeting other adults.

I did not agree with him when he said that, but as I continued my workout, I noticed that the thought of being on a large cruise ship by myself was sounding better and better. I began to wish that I had planned to go on the cruise alone.

After my workout, I went to pick up my son from his mom's house, so we could get on our way. He answered the door and immediately informed me that he had changed his mind; he would not be going on the trip after all, because he had absolutely no desire to be on a boat. After a few moments of disappointment, I realized how fast my thoughts had materialized; my wish to be on the cruise ship alone had come true.

Leaving Michael at home with his mom, I drove to the hotel where I was to spend the night before boarding. I had dinner by myself, and then went back to my room to relax and meditate.

During my meditation, the awareness came to me that I missed my son and really wished to have him with me on the cruise. I expressed the wish to my guide, who said that if I were sure about this, I should call my son at his mom's house in Las Vegas.

I called Michael the moment my meditation was finished. When he picked up the phone and realized who was calling, he confessed in a shaky voice that he missed me and had made a mistake in his decision.

I asked him if he would like to catch a plane in the morning and join me on the cruise, and he said he would. Once again, I was surprised by how fast my thoughts were materializing and my wishes were coming true.

I hung up, called the airline, and made arrangements for my son's morning flight from Las Vegas to Los Angeles. The next day was perfect; Michael's flight arrived on schedule, the drive to the cruise ship was effortless, and we boarded the ship with time to spare. I found myself truly happy to have my son with me, and our time spent together on the cruise was very joyous.

This whole experience reminded me that we have to be open to see how fast our thoughts can materialize and our wishes can come true.

I AM JUST THE MESSENGER

During meditation one morning, my mother—who has been one of my guides since her death—appeared with another woman who was wearing a turban.

I asked my mother who her friend was, and she replied, "This is Mrs. Bandar. She is the mother of your good friend, John Bandar." John and I had been good friends for nearly four years. He had come to America from Iran and was a reputable civil engineer in town.

Curious, I asked my mother what I could do for Mrs. Bandar.

She replied that Mrs. Bandar wished for me to give a message to her son.

Knowing John as I did, I was not sure that this was a very good idea. My mother heard my thoughts and replied in a firm voice, "Bijan, you are just the messenger; please avoid judgments."

I agreed to give John a message, and my mother said, "Mrs. Bandar wishes for you to tell John that today he must make a positive decision regarding a situation he has been procrastinating about for the past two years. The decision has to be made *today*." She emphasized that this message had to be given to John before noon.

After my meditation, I called John at his office. His secretary informed me that he was on the phone and had two other calls holding, so I left my name and number.

Knowing how busy John usually was, I thought it might be a day or two before he returned my call, but moments later the phone rang; to my surprise, it was John. He explained that—for some unknown reason—the phone lines in his office had gone dead, disconnecting his other calls just seconds before his secretary gave him my message.

With an uneasy feeling, I relayed the complete message that his mother had passed on to my mother. Laughing, he promised that by noon he would stop putting off his decision to enroll at the gym and work out with me.

I told him that was not what this was about. He was quiet for about two minutes and then asked me to repeat exactly what my mother had said. I told him again, recalling her words to the best of my ability.

His voice changed as he asked, "Do you swear on your son's life that she said that?"

"Yes," I replied. He thanked me and hung up.
John called me at home that evening, and after some small talk he explained to me that for the past two years he had been given the opportunity to become a

United States citizen; his mother's message had come on the last day of his eligibility. This surprised me; I thought he already was a citizen, since he had been here for so many years.

When I have the opportunity to pass on a message, my Ego seems to give me many reasons why I should not. But whenever I get my Ego out of the way and relay the message, I am always so very thankful for the results.

A MESSAGE FROM "OUR FRIEND"

In 1993, my guides began to give me a large number of messages that were for other people. I did not understand most of them, but acted as the messenger and passed them along anyway.

As I was meditating one morning, one of my guides named Moses informed me that I was supposed to give a message to Tom.

When I asked him who Tom was, my guide reminded me that Tom was a gentleman I had met at the gym the previous week. I was a little uncomfortable at the thought of giving him a message, since I did not know him very well. However, Moses assured me that it was going to be okay.

Reluctantly, I asked my guide what the message was. He told me to inform Tom that what he had been waiting the last eight months for would happen that afternoon, and that he should not take any additional steps in regard to it. I agreed to pass these words on, but reminded Moses that if I did not see Tom at the gym when I went there, or if it was going to be effortful, I would decline.

I went to the gym a short time after finishing my meditation and was pleased, though a little uneasy, to find Tom there.

After some small talk, I told him that I had a message for him. He was surprised and asked, "Who on Earth is sending a message to me?"

"Moses," I replied. "And he's not on Earth."

Tom laughed and sarcastically said, "Right. You know Moses."

When I explained to him that I meditated every morning, and that Moses was one of my guides, Tom asked me what "good ole Moses" had to say.

I repeated what Moses had told me, and Tom's face changed drastically. He lost his color, and for a moment I thought he was going to faint.

He asked me to repeat the message, so I did—exactly as it had been given to me. Then he asked, "Did Moses say anything else?" I told him no, then shook his hand and walked away.

Tom picked up his towel and followed me. "I don't feel like working out anymore," he said as he left the gym.

I saw Tom again about five days later. He ran up to me and gave me a warm, loving hug. He explained that he had followed the advice of Moses and everything had turned out perfectly. He thanked me and asked if I had any new messages for him. I shook my head.

Over the next three years, I usually saw Tom once or twice a week, and just about every time, with a great smile, he would ask me if there had been any news from *our friend.* To this day, I do not know what the message had meant to Tom, but I am glad I was able to be of service to him.

RELIVING HURTFUL EXPERIENCES

Whenever you have a hurtful experience, the best thing for you to do is simply acknowledge it, let the pain go, and release the memory. Release it, completely.

Of course, Ego does not wish for you to let go of any hurtful experience. Ego's power always comes from reliving the past, and so Ego wishes for you to experience the pain, over and over again. If Ego's power did not come from reliving past hurtful experiences, you would always choose to release the memory of pain, completely.

Each time that you listen to Ego, diving back into how or why something happened by describing and explaining it to others, you recreate it and bring it forth to be felt again. Unless you truly wish to relive the hurtful experience, you must let it go.

CHOOSING JOY OR FEAR

Do you have joy and laughter in your life, or do you have fear and anger? Do you like to watch happy movies and listen to people talking about their miracles, or are you drawn to fearful stories and news about disaster? If you can look at these choices and see which you are attracted to, you will know what creates your world around you.

If you are attracted to joy and light, your world is about peace. If you are attracted to fear and darkness, your world is about turmoil. You can change your world simply by being conscious of what you are attracted to.

Walk away from darkness and fear; it is not real anyway. Instead, be vigilant for the light. The light is your reality.

I AM NOT A BODY

Early in 1995, I was introduced to a book on out-of-body travel called *Journey To The Unknown,* written by Robert Monroe. I became fascinated by the subject, and read two of his other books: *Far Journey* and *Ultimate Journey.*

After reading these three books, I was even more fascinated by the subject. I felt a strong desire to experience out-of-body travel myself, so I enrolled in The Robert Monroe Institute in Virginia for two one-week sessions, back-to-back.

The atmosphere of both classes was delightful, and the trainers were more than kind and loving. I enjoyed my two weeks in Virginia tremendously. Along with meeting some great new friends, I experienced myself leaving my body on several occasions. It was exhilarating.

When I returned home, the thought of continuing the out-of-body experience was very much on my mind. I finally decided to consult my guide on the matter.

As soon as I went into my next meditation, my guide came to me. "Bijan," he said, "to leave your body and know that you can come back at any time is exciting, but it does not help you with your function, which is to heal. You did not come here to leave your body; you came to heal your mind. But if you ever truly wish to leave your body, simply tell me. I will take you and bring you back."

Since hearing those words from my guide, I have not intentionally left my body to accomplish a task. The most powerful lesson I learned from both the Monroe sessions and the consultation with my guide was that *I am not a body.* My perception of who I really am was changed completely.

WHATEVER YOU RESIST
WILL PERSIST

Whatever you think, you will bring forth; whatever you choose, you will experience. Whatever you resist will persist.

Whatever circumstances you think about, choose and then resist—or try to deny and separate yourself from—will grow. Whatever circumstances you think about, choose and then acknowledge—or allow and become one with—will disappear.

If you are in fear but you say, "I'm not afraid—everything is fine," you will become *more* frightened, not less. If you are in fear but you acknowledge, "I'm scared—I'm really frightened!" you will soon begin to laugh, and the fear will be released completely.

When you do not *resist* what you are feeling, but instead you are willing to *acknowledge* it and go through the experience, the feeling will lose its power over you. Then and only then will you be free to let the experience go—to release it and create a new experience.

RECOGNIZING A SAVIOR

In 1983, when I was living in Australia, I decided to visit my family in California for my vacation. Three days before returning to Australia, I attended a seminar with my best friend. Among the hundreds of people there, I noticed one particular woman. There was a tremendous energy between us. My friend and I sat next to her during the seminar, and later the three of us had breakfast together.

As we were all leaving the restaurant, my friend suggested that I give the woman a ride home. As it turned out, she and I spent the next three days together, effortlessly and joyfully. It was a very exciting time. There was intensity in the relationship that was quite remarkable.

One month after I returned to my home in Australia, the woman joined me there. Not long after this, she told me that she would like to have my son. A few months later Kathy and I were married—and in 1985, Michael was born.

When Michael was eight weeks old, the three of us returned to the mainland of the United States to live in Northern California. When Michael was six months old, Kathy and I separated; she moved to Las Vegas with Michael, and I moved to Southern California. In 1988 I also moved to Las Vegas, because I wished to be close to my son.

One day, when Michael was seven years old, I went to pick him up and Kathy refused to let me have him. I could see that she was in turmoil, so I let it go. After ten days of not seeing my son, my pain was tremendous. On several occasions I wept uncontrollably—I really missed him. Still, Kathy would not answer my telephone calls.

At the suggestion of a friend who was a frustrated divorced father, I attended a support group for fathers who were having difficulties with child custody. The anger in the meeting was almost overwhelming; I was astounded by the way in which these men referred to the mothers of their children. As I awaited a private consultation with the attorney who was offering advice, I realized that I was not where I wished to be, or where I should be. I knew I had a very strong case—I had paid my child support regularly—but this was not about being right or wrong.

I went home to cry and meditate, but my crying was so intense that I could not focus. In surrender, I decided to cry until I could cry no more, and finally, after releasing all of my pain, I experienced the profound sense of calmness which always leads me into meditation.

My guide came to me immediately. As soon as he spoke to me, I asked why I was being punished by such a horrible person. In answer, my guide offered a beautiful demonstration that became one of my most powerful miracles. He asked me if I recognized who Kathy was. When I said that I did not, my guide said that he would show me.

A circle of people, family, friends and others whom I loved, then surrounded me. Some I recognized, and some I did not. My guide said to the crowd, "Bijan desires to have a savior—someone who is not afraid to risk looking horrible to him. This might be someone he will actually hate. Is there anyone who loves Bijan enough to do this?"

To my astonishment, when I looked to see who would volunteer to be my savior, I saw that it was my ex-wife, Kathy. She said that she would be steadfast in the game until I got my lesson, and she would do this regardless of how much I might hate her.

As I saw Kathy in my meditation and heard her speak these words, my tears began to flow again, but for a different reason. I now understood the truth that Kathy was not my enemy at all, but rather, she was my savior. Instead of having anger about her, I now felt love for her.

When I ended the meditation and opened my eyes, the entire house appeared different. For some unknown reason, I walked directly to the telephone, and as I reached for it, it rang.

I knew it was Kathy even before I heard her voice. "Bijan," she said, "how long do you plan to keep your son waiting? He is impatient to see you." At first I was speechless, but when I regained my composure, I told her I would be right over.

This was an enormous relief for me. Of course I was happy to see my son, but I was even happier to have the absence of turmoil in my life. It was as if the weight had been completely lifted. Peace had returned. From that moment until this one, I have never been separated from my son.

UNCOVERING THE LIGHT

When I was born into this world, I was a light. I was very joyous, happy, and filled with shining love.

Then my Ego appeared, and as it grew, it started to attract things. Ego stuck things to me, and then stuck other things to those things, and so on; Ego likes to do that. These things were anything from wrong thoughts and love of material possessions, to fear, guilt, judgment, jealousy, resentment and anger. As more and more of this stuck to me, less and less light came through, until eventually I could see almost no light at all.

The principles I learned from studying *A Course in Miracles* and other quality thought systems, and the words that came through me from my guides to become the principles of *Absolutely Effortless Prosperity*, brought me in touch with how to remove this dark "stuff" surrounding my life. Now, my light shines brightly again.

GOING HOME TO PEACE

Shortly after completing the sessions at the Monroe Institute in 1995, I became very aware of my dreams. Every hour and a half, after full dream cycles, I would wake up and remember them vividly before sleeping again.

On one occasion, a dream was so powerful that I was unable to go back to sleep. It started with my meeting a man named Tom while I was walking with my brother, John. Tom told us that he could take us to an alien world in an instant, assuring us that we could return at any moment we desired. We were hesitant, but when he told us that our only function in that world would be to have a good time and be happy, we decided to go *at that instant.*

Almost immediately, we found ourselves in a magnificent green field that resembled a well-kept golf course. Warm sunshine fell upon the fruit trees that were all around us, and on a beautiful stream nearby. It was everything we had imagined heaven would be like.

As we walked around, laughing and gorging ourselves on the delicious fruit, I noticed several people sitting on the ground, guarding a few pieces of ordinary rock. I asked one of them what they were doing. "As you noticed," he replied, "this planet is covered with grass.

Rocks like these are very precious; to secure your future, you must have some of them underneath you."

Pointing to the fruit trees, I asked him, "With all of this food and fine weather, why do you wish to hold onto those rocks?"

"Because there is more to life than eating, drinking and being happy," he replied.

As we walked away, bewildered, I noticed a small rock a few feet in front of us. Quickly, I picked it up and showed it to my brother, John. After examining it, we decided to look for more rocks. It wasn't long before we were sitting next to each other, guarding the few pieces that we had found. We didn't know why we were doing this, but even though it was effortful, it felt normal.

I decided to count my rocks again, and a sense of fear and suspicion came over me as I realized that one of them was missing. "Maybe John snatched it away from me while I was not looking," I thought. Suspicion quickly turned to judgment and anger. Just as I was about to snatch my missing rock back from John's pile of rocks, Tom reappeared.

"It didn't take you long to adapt to the Ego of this planet," he said, smiling. "Have you forgotten that these rocks do not mean anything? Have you forgotten that you are here to laugh, be happy, and enjoy yourself?"

I told him that I did not feel peace here and wished to return home.

"When you are in peace, you *are* at home," Tom said. "If you wish to go home, just *choose peace.* It does not matter what planet you are on. You can choose peace or turmoil—heaven or hell—at every moment. The decision is yours: your peaceful home or your illusionary world."

Right at that moment I woke up. From that night on, I have gone home more often than I ever did before. I have not seen Tom since, but I will never forget him.

THE GAME OF LIFE

In Las Vegas, gaming tables and gambling are a common sight. Imagine that life is played on two gaming tables: one is the table of Spirit, and the other is the table of Ego. The chips that are won on Spirit's table are joy, peace, love, health, happiness, abundance and prosperity. The only chips that can be won on Ego's table are anger, turmoil, fear, disease, conflict, confusion and lack. The table that we choose to play on is, at every moment, up to us.

A female friend of mine once said to me, "Okay, I understand that I play on the table of Spirit, but my partner, who is my spouse, plays on the table of Ego. The only way that I am able to play with him is by going over to Ego's table."

My answer to that was, "Let him play on the table of Ego as long as he wishes to. He cannot play alone. If you are strong enough, patient enough, and loving enough—and if you do not leave the table of Spirit—sooner or later your spouse will get up, walk over to *your* table, and start playing there with you."

As long as we continue to give love, steadfastly refusing to allow Ego to get involved, others will have no choice but to come and play at our table. Once they play at Spirit's table, they can only walk away with the same things that we walk away with: joy, peace, love, health and abundance.

The most wonderful thing about playing at the table of Spirit is that everyone always wins and no one ever loses. On the table of Ego, however, everyone always loses and no one wins; whatever *appears* to be won at Ego's table is, in truth, not worth keeping.

PROSPERITY

I am one of four children from a very close family. Although we never had many material things while I was growing up, we shared a lot of love. I grew especially close to my younger brother John in those childhood years, and he continued to be a source of security for me as we grew into adulthood, just as I continued to be for him.

Because of our special bond, John and I were always willing to support one another in every way, including financially. I made it clear that whatever I had was available to him, and he repeatedly told me that I could rely on him for help of any kind, should I ever need it. I acknowledged this, and though I believed the privilege was one I would never have to exercise, its existence provided me with a feeling of security.

Ever since I had arrived in the United States at age nineteen, I always had money, yet I never recognized my financial wealth. Even when I became a millionaire at one time, I never considered myself prosperous.

My approach to prosperity was the traditional one: when I needed money, I would work harder. If my brother ever called for help with an investment, I was always able to accommodate him. Still, I never felt prosperous. The credit card companies apparently considered me to be a good risk, because they extended credit lines of over forty thousand dollars. I recall staring at the unused line of credit, thinking that maybe someday I should use it.

However, my security was short-lived. My income almost immediately evaporated as the bottom fell out of my business. Within six months, the thought of using the entire line of credit materialized.

Although I was working hard in real estate, deals were not coming together; I went for several months without a successful closing. I was forced to take out a second mortgage on my home, and my car had a note. I had used my credit cards to live on, and they were "maxed out."

I had less than one hundred dollars when, finally, it was time to play my "ace in the hole." I decided to call the one person who would help me without question or judgment: my brother John. I delayed contacting him as long as possible, hoping that something would come through. I had trouble sleeping as I worried about the money and when to call John. I knew that I had no alternative but to request his help.

I waited all day to make the call. John was very happy to hear from me, until I explained that I needed some money. His manner changed immediately—he became a businessman, not my generous and loving brother. He offered many excuses for why he could not give me the money. All the while, we both knew that he had it available. Although in the past I had loaned him as much as ninety thousand dollars at a time, he now thought that my request for five thousand dollars was excessive. Instead, he offered several hundred, "for food."

I explained that several hundred dollars would barely meet my obligations and that I would not have asked for five thousand if I did not need it. After I reminded John of the times I had assisted him, and after a lot of justification, he reluctantly agreed to send the money. I slept well that night, knowing that my brother was going to come through for me, just as I had known he would.

When I awoke the next morning, I noticed my telephone light blinking, telling me that I had a message. Although I was on my way to meditate, I decided to listen to it.

It was my brother John, recorded at 2 A.M. His voice sounded strange, very down, and lacking in energy. He said, "Bijan-jon (Persian for 'beloved Bijan'), I have not slept all night. I have come to the conclusion that I cannot help you. I have a family that I must think of first. I am very sorry."

I find it difficult to express how devastated I was—my brother had refused me when I needed his help. He was the one person I could rely on. I could not believe what I had heard. I replayed his message several times. I felt a total sense of panic, complete with chills and goose bumps. I was in shock.

I sought solace in meditation, but had difficulty letting go of my turmoil. I would wander around, get a drink of water, and then try again.

After nearly half an hour, I was finally able to meditate. My guide came to my assistance.

He said that I must be devastated. I told him that he was underestimating the situation. He asked me if I wished to be at peace. "Most certainly," I replied. He then asked me what my brother was to me. I answered, "My brother."

"No," my guide said, "you have made your brother a god. When you needed help, you turned to *him,* not to your Father. Don't you understand that it takes much more effort to turn to your brother for help, rather than to God? God's gifts and God's help are available to you just for the asking, without effort on your part. The Father says that if we ask with conviction and faith, we shall <u>always</u> receive without effort."

I could not believe what I was hearing. "That easily?" I asked.

"Just that easily," he replied.

"Then, will I be okay?" He told me that I was always okay. "Do I need to do anything?" He assured me that I needed to do nothing. Relieved and peaceful, I moved to stop my meditation.

"Where are you going, Bijan?" my guide asked. "Your work is just beginning."

"But you just told me that I need to do nothing," I said.

"Bijan," my guide said, "I am going to explain to you the nature of prosperity. For you to learn this lesson, I had to take some things away from you, and for the benefit of your lesson, your beloved brother John was in total turmoil. You are not to hesitate in healing and forgiving; you are to communicate with John immediately and extend your love."

With joy I telephoned my brother. His voice reflected an exhausted being. He began by telling me that he did not know why he had done what he had to me. "I am willing to help total strangers," he said, "but I cannot understand why I would ever hesitate to help the one who is so close to me."
He was sincerely saddened and offered his financial assistance in whatever amount.

I began to describe my miracle, not certain that he would understand; his frame of reference was very different from mine. He quietly listened as I outlined my lesson. I thanked him for his help in my growth and told him that I loved him.

Again, he offered his financial help. I explained that he had already helped me so much, and everything was okay; I would not need his financial support after all. To my surprise and delight—and to my relief—he said that he understood.

Within days, the most unlikely real estate deals began to close. Within weeks, my credit cards were completely paid off, and within a few months, my car note and second mortgage were paid in full. Without effort on my part, but with complete enjoyment, deals were closing quickly and easily.

Since that time, my relationship with my brother has become even stronger. I love him fully as my brother, not as a god, and I am greatly privileged to have him in my life. To this day, I am a very prosperous person.

EXPANDING MY PROSPERITY

I received a telephone call one day from an Arabian gentleman named Mustafah. He was interested in having me weight-train his son. After a couple of meetings, Mustafah asked me if I would work with him on some property deals. He was a prince of Arabia and had plenty of money coming to him, so I agreed without a second thought. Before I knew it, we had several big deals in escrow. Some of the commissions were more than I had ever dreamed of making, and the work was absolutely effortless.

This continued for many months, but the story was always the same; there were never any closings. I simply could not understand why none of the deals closed, and repeatedly asked my guide, "What is the reason for this? The work is effortless and the commissions are bigger than I ever imagined!" Each time that I asked my guide, he listened, chuckled softly, and replied that I simply was not ready for the answer yet.

Then one day Mustafah told me that because of the exchange of currency and the delay of his funds, he was in need of some quick cash. Knowing he was a wealthy prince of Arabia, I offered him what I had in the bank, which was three thousand dollars. He graciously accepted and promised that he would pay it off within a few days. Unfortunately, he did not.

Again I asked my guide, "What is the reason for this? Mustafah is a prince of Arabia with more money than I could ever imagine having. Why is it that he does not pay me back?" My guide's reply was that I simply was not ready for the answer yet.

Finally, after a year of setting up property deals for Mustafah and watching his escrows fall through, I removed myself from his presence. We still kept in touch about once a week, but that was the extent of our relationship. I continued to ask my guide if I was ready to hear the answer to my question, and he continued to tell me I was not ready. Finally, I let go of the question, let go of Mustafah, and opened myself to manifesting successful property deals elsewhere.

About two years later, my guide finally told me the reason for this encounter. "Bijan," he said, "Mustafah came into your life to show you that large amounts of money are available to you without effort; it is just as effortless to have a lot of money as it is to have a little. All that matters is that you *believe* it is possible, and you *know* that you deserve it. Even though you were prosperous before meeting Mustafah, he was the main reason you were able to extend your abundance and worthiness far beyond what it had ever been."

It is such freedom to realize the truth: Mustafah was one of the angels in my life.

WEAKENING THE EGO

As Spirit within me becomes more empowered by my vigilance for joy, peace and light in my life, my Ego becomes weaker and weaker. I am no longer faced with the conflicts and turmoil that my Ego used to thrive on when meeting another Ego, because my Ego knows that it no longer has my power behind it to win.

As the saying goes, "It takes two to tango." Giving more power to my Spirit has resulted in no conflicts with other Egos.

HOW PROSPERITY WORKS

We had been examining the idea of prosperity for several weeks during our seminar on *A Course in Miracles*, when a man asked me to meet with him after class. He was involved in two businesses and now wished to launch a third, but was in turmoil over his prosperity.

The man asked me to back him with several thousand dollars for his new venture. His new business was not one in which I wished to be involved, but his request did give me the opportunity to explain the way prosperity works in our lives.

I told him that prosperity does not necessarily mean that we have hundreds of thousands of dollars sitting idly in the bank; prosperity is not about greed or excess, and it is not about *doing* anything to *create* anything. In truth, prosperity is about *feeling* worthy and deserving, being open to receive, and knowing that everything we desire will be provided for us. Someone who has millions of dollars is not prosperous if he still has fear and turmoil. I may have only a few hundred dollars in the bank, but I am truly prosperous. When I desire something, it is always available to me.

MIRACLES ARE NOT SIZED

As I sat down to write a check for my mortgage payment one morning, I had to admit that paying off a mortgage was not one of my favorite pastimes. When I meditated that day, I told my guide that my life was wonderful and that I was living without effort. "…except for one thing," I said. "This request would require a *big* miracle."

"There are no big or small miracles," my guide interrupted. "Miracles are not sized. What is it you desire?" I told him that I wished for my house mortgage to be paid. He said it would be done.

For years I had been trying to sell a particular piece of commercial property, with no success—but now a buyer unexpectedly appeared out of nowhere, and the property sold within two months. My commission on the sale was one-hundred-four thousand dollars.

At first I was puzzled by the amount because it exceeded my mortgage. Then I recognized—with the help of my CPA—that the excess money covered the taxes on my commission.

A LESSON IN FORGIVENESS

Tony is an old friend of mine whom I have known for over twenty years. A few years ago, he asked me to sell his business for him. The very next day, another friend of mine, Karim, asked me if I had any businesses for sale. When I told him about Tony's business, he was very interested and made a full-price offer. Tony was elated; he had been willing to accept much less than what he had been asking. We had a deal. My net commission upon closing would be seventy-five hundred dollars.

A few weeks later, Tony was supposed to meet us at the property and show the business books to Karim. For some reason, however, he did not show up. We made several more appointments to meet, but each time, Tony stood us up. Finally, Karim said that if the seller did not wish to sell the business, he was willing to back out.

The deal fell through. However, my broker decided that since we had procured a willing and able buyer, we were still entitled to our commission. He then hired an attorney to initiate a lawsuit. When the attorney called me to take my statement, I explained to him that I was unwilling to participate in the lawsuit against Tony. I did not wish to have the commission under those circumstances, and had already forgiven Tony for his behavior. I called my broker to tell him of my decision.

Later that day, an Asian woman whom I had never seen before came to our firm. She walked straight into my broker's office, and I heard them arguing for half an hour.

Needing to ask my broker something that could not wait, I decided to interrupt them. When I opened the door and walked in, the woman stared at me and asked in a very heavy accent, "What is your name?" I told her my name was Bijan. She then said to me, "I see in you that you are going to sell my shopping center." My broker turned to me with a surprised look and explained that she had come here to cancel her listing, which he had accepted six months earlier, but had been unable to sell. Then, the woman announced to him, "Bijan has the exclusive listing on my property."

What happened next was amazing; I accepted the listing, and within forty-eight hours I had a buyer for the woman's property. The deal closed in forty-five days and my net commission was seventy-five thousand dollars!

I knew that by giving up my resentment and grievances against Tony, and by completely forgiving him, I had literally multiplied my receiving by ten. Although he was not aware of the role he had played in my lesson of forgiveness, I was very grateful to Tony.

ASKING FOR WHAT YOU WANT

Shortly after I had paid off my automobile, it started to require repairs. The problems were not major, but they were consistent and annoying. Every time there was another problem, I experienced turmoil and said to myself, "Why is this happening to me? I don't deserve this."

Finally I recalled some very good words of advice that my guide had given me in the past: simply to ask the Universe for what I wanted. I truly desired to get rid of my old automobile and decided to ask for a new one. During my next meditation, while I was giving a very involved explanation of why my car was an annoyance, my guide interrupted me. "Bijan," he said, "please leave the story behind and get to the bottom line. What is it that you desire?"

I thought for a moment and then told him that I wished to have a new car. He asked what type and how much. I said I did not know, but that I would like a four-wheel-drive vehicle. He told me to come to him with definite information, not with a vague request.

Over the next few days, I drove all types of four-wheel-drive trucks, including a Samurai, a Pathfinder, a Jeep and a Four Runner. Finally, I went back to my guide and told him that I liked the Four Runner best, and that it would cost twenty-four thousand dollars. My guide told me that it was done.

Within one month, I had a closing on a real estate deal in which I had put very little effort. The deal was unexpected—a gift—and my commission was exactly twenty-four thousand dollars.

While driving to the dealership to purchase the Four Runner, my Ego became very active. It kept telling me to remember that I had been in heavy debt only shortly before this, so perhaps I should buy a Jeep and save six thousand dollars—or buy a Samurai and save twelve thousand dollars.

Suddenly I was in turmoil again, wondering if I truly deserved to spend all my commission on the Four Runner, or if I should save some of the money in case I might need it for something important.

Then I began to laugh at myself. Even though *I* had learned my lesson and was now coming from prosperity, my *Ego* was still coming from scarcity! Ego's arguments were strong but ineffective; I ignored them, and purchased the Four Runner.

REMEMBERING MY SOURCE

One day while I was living in Australia, I walked to a beautiful park to eat my lunch. I had brought an extra loaf of bread with me, to feed the birds.

As I sat down on one of the benches, a half-dozen crows landed in front of me, looking for a handout. I reached into my bag for a slice of bread and threw it onto the ground. All of the crows hungrily dove for it, but the first one that reached it snatched the whole slice and flew away with it. Immediately, the other crows took off, chasing the crow with the bread.

I rose and hurriedly tossed the rest of the bread onto the ground, whistling and shouting to call the crows back, but they were determined to get a piece of that stolen slice. Bewildered, I sat down on the bench, wondering why they had panicked over one slice of bread and could not even see that I had thrown enough on the ground for all of them.

As I thought about their behavior, a feeling of peace came over me; I had just learned a profound lesson. At every moment, I can choose to be like the crows and continually ignore my source while trying to grab scraps from others, or I can choose to let go of my fear of scarcity, knowing that God is my source. At every moment, I can allow fear to lead me toward thoughts of scarcity, or I can allow love to remind me that there is always plenty for me and for others to receive.

When I left the park after finishing my lunch, all of the bread was still on the ground; no crows had returned. Since that day, I have seen everyone's prosperity in a different light.

FORGIVING OTHERS
TO FORGIVE MYSELF

As a real estate agent, I have worked with many different types of people. One time, I placed an ad in the newspaper for the sale of some land. A man who responded to the ad recognized that I spoke with an accent, and asked my nationality. When I told him that I was Persian, he began a discussion of the land for sale, in my native language.

He told me that he had recently moved to Las Vegas from Hawaii, where he owned several businesses. He also owned a nursing home in Las Vegas and had a substantial amount of cash that he wished to invest in this area.

I arranged to take him to lunch. During lunch, he ordered a full meal and several beers. Afterward, we continued to look at properties until dinnertime. Again, he told me that he was hungry, and I took him for another meal. As an agent who specializes in rather large land transactions, I am accustomed to taking clients out to eat while putting together land deals, so I wasn't disturbed by his behavior.

During our conversation, he told me that he was fluent in twelve languages and had degrees in law, dentistry and oral surgery. He told me that be-cause he spoke many languages, and because of his educational background, he had been employed by the United Nations before his move to Hawaii. As a person who was born in another country, I often meet people who have acquired higher degrees in their native land, then come to the United States and begin another career. During the process, they learn many different languages. He was well-spoken and very knowledgeable. I was honored to be with him and to be of service to him.

Over the next five or six days, our routine remained the same. I would pick him up for breakfast, and we would look at land, go to lunch, search for more land, and finish with dinner. At no time did he offer to pay for anything. In fact, he mentioned that my commission on the sale of the land would far exceed the cost of the meals. Several times he asked me to stop at various places so that he could run personal errands, as well.

The perfect deal finally materialized. I wrote up the offer and he gave me a check for ten thousand dollars as a deposit.

As I was driving to the escrow company, he telephoned me on my cellular phone. He told me that he had cancelled the check and did not wish to go ahead with the transaction. I froze.

My telephone rang again, and this time it was my girlfriend. When I told her what had happened, she began to laugh at me. I was not pleased. She explained that the man was an accomplished con artist. As a student of *A Course in Miracles,* I looked for the lesson in all of this, but nothing occurred to me. I became angry and upset.

That night I could not sleep; this is very unusual for me. The fact that I had been misled—not for one day, but for an entire week—was very disturbing.

After a restless night, I went to my meditation pyramid with a *big* attitude. One of my guides appeared, laughing at me. I was not amused, and demanded to know what was so funny.

After more laughter, my guide said, "You do not see it, do you?" I explained that I had looked at everything and that there was nothing to see; there was no lesson for me. He suggested that we look at it together.

He asked what bothered me most about the experience. As I struggled to control my temper, I told him that the man had lied to me about speaking twelve languages.

My guide asked me to remember the first day that I had arrived in the United States. A woman had asked me how many languages I spoke. I had replied that I spoke six languages, in an attempt to impress her.

My guide asked me if that had been true. I told him that it hadn't; I only spoke Persian and marginal English at the time.

He began to laugh again, and said, "See, he doubled the number of languages that he speaks, so that you could recognize your error and rid yourself of the guilt you have carried for many years. By forgiving him, you forgive yourself."

Only partially relieved, I continued with an outraged reminder that he had claimed to have three graduate degrees. After more laughter, my guide asked me to remember my first return trip to Persia—when I had told my family and friends that I was an engineer.

Again, my guide asked if *that* had been true. I responded that it hadn't, because I was only in my first year of college at that time. Until that moment, I had completely forgotten about *that* one. My guide resumed his laughter and said, "He *tripled* his degrees, so that you could see your error and rid yourself of the guilt!"

Feeling a little embarrassed, I went on to ask about the exaggeration of his cash holdings. By this time, my guide was not laughing and asked me to remember another incident…. This continued until I was in total peace. No longer did I view the client as a con man, but as an angel who had come to rid me of my guilt.

That afternoon, I called my angel and invited him to dinner that evening. I dined with him without animosity or anger, for I saw him in a completely different light—as a *savior.* When we parted after dinner, I felt complete with him and at peace with myself.

Shortly after that evening, I telephoned him. He had totally disappeared, without a trace.

CAUSE AND EFFECT

Your thoughts are the causes that produce effects which become your reality. What you see outside of yourself is only the effect of your thinking. Instead of working to change the effect, it is important to work on your thoughts—on your mind. Only at *this* level can change be made to produce a different effect.

Whenever you produce an effect that you no longer desire, it is very important that you accept it as an effect of your own thoughts. Only by *accepting and releasing it* can you be free to create a *different* effect.

For example, suppose that you had created a chair, but now decide that you no longer desire the chair, but desire a table instead. You must first accept and release the chair—the effect of your thought—before you are free to go back to your mind and create a table.

You can always change the reality outside of yourself by changing your mind about it, and thereby changing the cause.

HONESTY

Sometime in 1994, I found a piece of land for a dear friend to purchase, but a few months later he called and asked me to help him sell it. He said that he was willing to take up to a forty percent loss, just to have a write-off. I understood his urgency and agreed to sell the property.

As we hung up, I realized that the deal was too good to pass up, and decided that I would like to buy the land myself. This would help both of us at the same time; he would have his write-off and I would have a profitable land deal.

However, I was reluctant to make him an offer, and struggled with my reluctance for days. I felt that I would be taking unfair advantage of his situation by purchasing the land far below market value and then turning around to sell it for the real value.

When my friend and I met again, I explained that I had spent many hours putting together a deal that would enable *me* to purchase the land. Though I had expected him to be angry and disappointed in me as a friend, his response was just the opposite. He looked at me in awe and said he wished that *he* could be as honest as I was. At that point, we postponed making any decision about the land; instead we spoke at length about honesty and the importance of being truly open with everyone in our lives.

The very next day I received a call from someone who wished to buy my friend's property. The offer was twice the amount he had been willing to sell it for, and instead of taking a forty percent loss, he would be making a twenty percent profit! I could not help but tease him as I extended the contract to him with joy.

Through this experience, we both made money and we each learned a great lesson: when we are open and honest, Spirit has the opportunity to bring peace and profit.

THE BEAUTY OF THE PRESENT

During my first visit to Australia after my mother's death, I wandered around my sister's ranch, completely filled with turmoil. Issues of prosperity, combined with homesickness and sadness over my mother's physical absence, overwhelmed me. My mind raced from one perceived problem to another; from one area of discontent to the next.

But then, within the space of a single moment, I consciously let go of all past and future issues and surrendered myself to the present. I totally altered the chaos that surrounded me. In doing so, I recognized that there were no past or future complications; indeed, there was only the present.

In that moment, I became aware of the world around me. The beauty of the sights, sounds and smells was totally and completely overpowering. It was as though I was seeing nature in all of its splendor for the first time.

In the present, there had been no room for those things of the past, because they did not exist; I had created them. In that creation, I had blocked the incomparable beauty of the present.

GRATEFUL SURRENDER

As time went on after our divorce, Kathy and I came to a very comfortable arrangement regarding the custody of our son, Michael. Five days each week, she brought him to my home at six o'clock in the evening; Michael would spend the night, and I would return him to Kathy early the following morning. This gave each of us special time with our son. I truly appreciated the five nights I had with Michael, and though Kathy had him with her every day, I understood and honored how much she cherished her two nights with him.

At one point, though, I wished to take Michael to a special event that fell on one of those two nights. When I telephoned Kathy to ask if he could join me for this one evening, I was greeted by a very angry mother. She went into great detail as to why I should not disturb their valued time together.

My usual approach would have been to explain patiently why this was a special opportunity, and to persuade her to come to my way of thinking. But now, without a deliberate attempt to form the words, I found myself saying, "You are right. I am sorry. It will not happen again."

We said goodbye and I hung up the telephone. I was pleased when I recognized that I was not trying to control the situation.

After about three minutes, the telephone rang. It was Kathy. She resumed her explanation, wanting me to fully understand how what I had done was inappropriate, and exactly why I should not have done it. Again, I apologized and humbly hung up the telephone.

Again the telephone rang, and again it was Kathy. This time she wanted me to understand that she was not trying to be mean to me, but did need to make it perfectly clear that I was not to interfere with her time with Michael—under *any* circumstances. I said that I fully understood, and apologized again.

I hung up the telephone, and again the telephone rang. This time she asked me if I really wanted to see him so much that I would disturb their time together. I told her, quite sincerely, that I had made a mistake, I was very sorry, and that it would not happen again.

After another five minutes, the telephone rang again. She said, "Pick him up in about ten minutes…but you realize that he doesn't have time to take a shower." I gratefully thanked her, and then picked up Michael. As I drove away with him, I realized once again that by surrendering control, what I desired was given to me without effort.

EXCITEMENT IN THE PRESENT

Whenever I am in the present—which is Truth and the only reality—I notice that it is very quiet. Ego says this is very boring, for nothing is happening, but it is really very exciting! The present is about *being*, and when I am there—without my Ego and my perception of what the present should be like—I am in a place of peace, joy and love. When I go beyond, to where Truth is, I am where I really desire to be.

SERVING MY OWN BEST INTEREST

Prior to starting *A Course in Miracles*, I had studied many enrichment programs that promote seizing control. This is an effective tool for establishing goals, persuading people, and ultimately for getting your way. However, *A Course in Miracles* teaches that only by relinquishing control to Spirit, will I allow my own best interest to be served. Unfortunately, old habits die hard.

For years, I have regularly gone to a gym to work out. One day, an attractive woman on the Stairmaster caught my eye. I smiled and said, "Hello."

She frowned and muttered a hello in return.

The next day, the same thing happened, but with a different woman. This time, she was even more attractive. Again, I greeted her—and again, I received a scowl and a subdued hello.

My Ego began a campaign. It reminded me of all the control classes I had taken and encouraged me to go for what I wanted. I surrendered. I jumped on the adjacent Stairmaster and began small talk. After half an hour, I asked the woman if she would join me for dinner that evening, and she accepted. I was successful! I had gone for it and won. But what had I won?

During dinner, I quickly discovered that we had very little in common. She smoked, used profanity at every opportunity, and retreated to the rest room frequently. When she returned each time, she had difficulty with her nose.

Halfway through dinner, I had a raging headache. During one of her rest room visits, I declared to my guide, "Do not *ever* listen to me! Give me *only* what is in my best interest, *not what I ask for!*" After dinner, I used my headache as an excuse to cut our date short and take her home.

The next day at the gym, I walked by the Stairmaster and said hello to the woman using it. It was not my intention to date her; in truth, I was just giving her an absentminded greeting.

When she frowned at me and barely said hello, I started to laugh inside. I thanked my guide for my lesson—such a complete one.

SHARING THE LESSONS OF OTHERS

During my seven years of studying and teaching *A Course in Miracles*, I continuously expanded my consciousness. On one particular evening, an event happened in our class that brought a lot of light to me.

A few minutes before the end of the session, a friend of mine named Shelly rushed in. She was determined to share her miracle that evening. The class was very full and there were many people still sharing.

Finally, it was Shelly's turn. As she excitedly began to speak, another participant named Hannah interrupted and said, "I'm sorry Shelly, but class is over now. We can't listen to your miracle tonight."

Everyone was very surprised. Hannah's abruptness seemed out of character—she was a very gentle soul who had a deep love for everyone. I could feel Shelly's disappointment and anger as she rushed out of the room.

Class ended as usual, and as everyone exchanged hugs, Hannah came over to me and broke down crying in my arms. "What have I done?" she asked. "What would make me so mean to Shelly? Why didn't I give her the opportunity to share?"

"God works in mysterious ways," I said. "Many times, things that we believe are hurtful are really done for our own best interest. When we open our minds to the knowledge that there is always another way to view any experience in life, we can begin to recognize everything as good."

Five days later, I received a phone call from Shelly. I could hear the excitement in her voice. "I've been in so much turmoil since I left that night," she said. "But I just got off the phone with my friend Nancy, and now I realize that what happened that night was really a miracle for me! When Nancy asked me how I reacted when I couldn't share my miracle, I told her that I felt totally out of control and so I just ran away. Then Nancy asked me, 'But isn't that what you do with all of your relationships whenever you feel out of control?'"

By this time, Shelly was weeping with joy. "All these years I never understood why my relationships failed. I am so thankful for having been at your class that night, and for the confrontation with that wonderful woman. She helped me to bring my awareness to a level where I could finally see the truth. I'd like to phone her and express my deepest gratitude…I'm sure she doesn't realize what she did for me."

While I was giving her Hannah's number, I became aware that there was a beautiful lesson in all of this for me, too. When I come from love, it does not matter what the circumstances may look like to me; there is always a profound effect on someone else's life as well as on mine. In every action, there is always a lesson for someone. I no longer concern myself with the outcome; I simply remind myself to *trust God.*

SURRENDERING CONTROL

I am routinely reminded of the advantages of surrendering control. One time, for example, I purchased two finches—a male and a female— with the intention of breeding them. The next morning, to my surprise, both finches were singing. This was a surprise to me because female finches do not sing.

Immediately I telephoned the gentleman who had sold the birds to me, and explained the situation. I was eager to resolve the problem and hoped to replace one of the males with a female as soon as possible.

The gentleman told me that he had a doctor's appointment in ninety minutes. I was about to convince him that, if I hurried, I could make it to his house quickly enough for him to exchange the bird and still arrive at his appointment on time, but before I spoke, I caught myself. Instead, I agreed to meet him later in the afternoon, as he suggested. I was actually surprised by my response, since I firmly believed that I had plenty of time to go to his house and make the exchange.

After we finished speaking, I received a telephone call from a client that I thought was scheduled for an appointment later in the day. The gentleman reminded me that I was to see him in fifteen minutes. This was a very important two-part real estate meeting, and I had written only the second half of the meeting in my planner.

Had I insisted upon controlling the time to exchange the finches, I would have been unavailable to attend this important and profitable meeting.

SEEING THE TRUTH ABOUT MYSELF THROUGH OTHERS

A short while after beginning the study of *A Course in Miracles*, I had the opportunity to heal my perception of a colleague. I was not very happy working with him, and never felt good about myself when I was in his presence. There seemed to be only two choices available to me: leave the company, or stay and get along with him. I chose to stay with the company, and asked my guide for help.

"Imagine that you are a loving father with a lot of children, or a master with many loyal students," he said. "When a child or a student comes to you asking for help or calling for love, what do you do?"

"Now," he continued, "think of every person you meet or have contact with as your child or your student who is asking, 'Who am I?' Your function in this world is to see beyond every person's behavior and remind each one who he or she really is—a powerful child of God and a light of the world. As each one will know this Truth, he or she will mirror back to you who you really are, as well. You cannot do it by yourself."

The very next day, I found myself excited about going to work and healing my perception of this individual. When I arrived at my office and was imagining him verbally attacking me, to my surprise, all that I saw was a loving person who just wished to share his love and light with me in the best way that he could. Since that moment, I have found him to be funny and joyous; I have felt very peaceful in his presence.

LOVE OR DISCIPLINE

When my son Michael was about four years old, he would often come to visit. His method of getting my attention was to pull my ears, grab my clothes, and annoy me. When this behavior became intolerable, I would regain control with the age-old technique of shaking him harshly for a moment.

One night, Michael began repeating his pattern of misbehaving. As I held him in the moment before shaking him, a beautiful miracle occurred. I felt my real self only as unconditional love.

Instead of shaking Michael, I drew him close to me. As I looked into his eyes, I told him that I loved him and kissed him softly on the forehead. This behavior was totally unprecedented, for we had always shared a "macho" relationship.

My son's response was equally unusual. He gently caressed my cheek with his chubby little hand. We gazed deeply into each other's eyes as we wept.

Slowly, my son's physical body began to fade, and as I held him, he was transformed into a bright light. It seemed as though we were in that moment for an eternity. Since then, my relationship with Michael has been permanently altered. I no longer need to control him with physical means.

JUDGMENT

At the end of either the second or third *A Course in Miracles* meeting I attended, I noticed that one of the ladies was using the study book as a footrest. This was uncomfortable for me because I felt that it was disrespectful to treat the book in this manner. I saw it as holy—like the Bible, the Torah or the Koran. Finally, I approached the woman and said, "Using the book in this way is very disrespectful because it contains the word of God."

She smiled and replied, "That is your perception."

I really did not understand what she was saying, so I continued, insisting that she should apologize, pick up the book, and treat it with more respect.

Again she smiled and said, "It is only a book."

It took me a while to realize what she meant. With my judgment, I make things *more* or *less* important. When the name of God is in a book, only *my* judgment can make the book holier than anything or anyone else. Through this experience, I noticed that once I clear my judgment out of the way, everything is equal and perfect.

TRAFFIC MIRACLES

One day, while driving the freeway in Las Vegas, I pulled behind some very slow traffic in one of the exit lanes. As the traffic in my lane began to move again, a car in the fast lane suddenly pulled into the few feet of space that opened between my car and the vehicle in front of me. I barely stopped in time to avoid hitting him, and consequently, the vehicle behind me barely missed my car.

I was outraged! Surely my anger was not the appropriate response, so I asked my guide, "What is the lesson in all of this?"

I heard a voice clearly say, "Look at the driver in front of you."

As I looked, I could see that he was trying very hard not to glance at me in his rear view mirror. Again I asked, "Please clarify this."

The voice said, "Remember last week, when you were in a hurry and pulled in front of someone?"

I remembered that incident clearly, and that I was also trying very hard not to glance at the driver behind me in my rear view mirror. As I opened my vision, I could see that every incident that occurred on that off-ramp had been *me* at one time or another.

The voice concluded by saying, "If you give up worrying about time, you will realize how perfect everything in the Universe is."

Since that day, I have changed my perception. I find that whenever I am in that slow lane, I gladly open a space and give way to "myself in another car." In fact, I go out of my way to smile and show forgiveness to "myself in the other car" whenever I do something that is inconsiderate. Life is great when you get in touch with who you are!

REMEMBERING MY GOAL

I was Mr. Universe, Natural Division, in 1993 and 1994. I trained for the competitions and looked good. In November of 1995, I represented the United States at the World Cup of Bodybuilding, Natural Division, in Australia. I finished in second place; first place went to an Australian. When he was named the winner, I was very happy for him—after all, it was his home and he had many friends and relatives at his competition.

I returned to Las Vegas and continued to train. As the Mr. Universe competition in December approached, I was confident that I would win again. With the additional training and preparation for Australia, I had never looked better.

When I went to the prejudging for the competition in California, I realized that there were two men who would finish ahead of me. As a former judge, I knew the criteria for winning, yet I was convinced they had used steroids. I was angry, tired and not my usual enthusiastic self.

After the prejudging, my son Michael and I returned to our room, and I asked him to be quiet while I meditated. My guide came to me quickly, and I explained to him that I was feeling weak and very upset. I was confused by the events of the day, believing that I was being cheated. I asked my guide how I could have won the title last year, but might lose it this year.

He asked me what my goal was in this world, and I responded without hesitation, "Peace." Then he asked me if I had altered my goal, and immediately I understood: my goal *now* was to be Mr. Universe. My guide explained to me that if I won this year, I would continue to pursue the Mr. Universe title. I suddenly realized that in my quest to be Mr. Universe, I had sacrificed my peace. If we live in turmoil, we do not miss peace, but if we have known peace, its absence is profound.

After my meditation, I felt strong, happy and peaceful. Although I normally do not eat between the prejudging and the finals, Michael and I went out for a big Persian feast.

When we returned, I sought out the two men who I thought would finish ahead of me. I told them that they looked magnificent and *should* win the competition. They were shocked at my attitude change, and my son was even more puzzled! He said that I was a totally different person from who I had been at the prejudging. It is so great to be at peace.

GIFT FROM A FRIEND

My longtime best friend shared a story with me which illustrates, very clearly, the importance of our point of view.

One Friday, while driving, he noticed a hitchhiker. Although he was not in the habit of stopping for hitchhikers, when he saw that it was a woman alone, he offered her a ride.

As they chatted, he realized how much they had in common, and noticed that she was very pretty. He asked her if she would like to have something to eat, and she accepted.

After dinner, he drove her to her neighborhood. She said that she did not want her mother to worry about her hitchhiking, so she asked him to drop her off down the street.

He asked if she would like to see him again. She said that she was busy over the weekend, but that he could call her on Monday.

Throughout the weekend, he was very happy in anticipation of seeing her again. The more he thought about her, the lovelier she became.

On Monday, he waited until the afternoon to call her. When he dialed the number, he was greeted with the recording, "This number is no longer in service."

Later, when he told me the story, I expressed dismay at how disappointed he must have felt.

He chuckled and explained to me that he had two choices. Certainly, he could have dwelt upon disappointment, but instead, he chose to bless her for the pleasant weekend he had spent in anticipation of seeing her again. It was all in his point of view—in his outlook. She was still a lovely lady.

HAVING GOALS

Because this world is very goal oriented, it would seem impossible to live and flourish without having them. As a result, we are always setting various goals for ourselves to achieve, and then working toward achieving them. We work, compare and judge; we set priorities about which goal is more important than another. There may be a sense of joy when one goal is reached, but it is often cancelled out by a sense of discontent, because another goal is unfulfilled. So then we set more goals and work to achieve them, following the same pattern again and again. We have forgotten that there is only one goal to choose.

When we choose peace as our only goal, everything that we desire in order to achieve that goal of peace will be provided. If we desire good health to have peace, then good health will be ours. If we desire a great relationship to have peace, then a great relationship will also be provided for us.

Remember that God gives us whatever we desire, so we always reach our goal. What is most important is our choice of which goal to pursue. We can choose effort and turmoil, or we can choose peace. To have a joyous and effortless life, our only goal must be peace.

GIFTS FROM THE FATHER

My son Michael asked me for a new video game that was the talk of all the boys in school. He said that he would be forever grateful if I would get it for him. His deep desire and persistence made me more than happy to buy the game, but what I noticed after he had it was that he soon began to spend most of his waking hours playing with it. He no longer had time for homework, daily chores or me.

When I asked my guide what approach would be best for correcting my son, he asked me, "What is Michael doing that you do not like?" I replied that he had made a god out of his video game. My guide smiled and said, "Isn't that what you do with most of the gifts that you receive from your Father? You are very persistent in getting what you wish to have—and you wish to have it all. With deep desire, you always say, 'I will be forever grateful if you give me this gift.' Soon after you have it, however, you make the gift your god."

"This is not only true with Ego's wishes," he added. "It is also true when you receive the part of your inheritance that is prosperity, health, and effortless relationships. You serve these gifts so loyally that you forget about your Father. Remember that your goal is peace, while your function in this world is to heal yourself and others." Once again, an experience with my son had taught me a lesson.

PROJECTING MY GUILT

My ex-wife Kathy and I were together for about three years. She is a magnificent person, and I have learned many lessons from her. One lesson that I clearly remember was about projecting guilt.

For a time during our marriage, we lived with my mother in Australia. One day, when I came home from the gym, I found my mother in the kitchen. She had just returned from the market, and as I approached her, I noticed that she was washing the plastic grocery bags to reuse them. A sense of disappointment came over me; I thought to myself, "With all of the money that I make and the income that she receives, why would she have to do that?"

I was just about to scold her when Kathy entered the kitchen. She took one look at my face and asked, "What's the matter? Why are you so upset?" I told her about my mother washing the plastic grocery bags, and my feelings about this.

Kathy listened to my long story and began to laugh. I was not amused. Then she reminded me of an incident that had occurred two days earlier. We were in the kitchen putting away groceries when my mother walked in. My mother saw that I was holding an empty plastic grocery bag, and quickly said, "Don't throw that away!" The moment I heard those words, my Ego stepped in; I'd had every intention of saving the bag, but now I said, "Mother, we don't need to save these," and I threw it in the trash.

Remembering this incident, I smiled at Kathy and acknowledged the miracle of the lesson. I had just become upset with my mother because I was not feeling good about myself saving grocery bags the way *she* always did. We had both been brought up in a place of scarcity, but now I felt guilty about it. Not wanting or liking this guilt, I was projecting it onto my mother. Only by seeing my guilt in someone else, was I able to bring it up to be healed in me.

Now that I understood this, I was easily able to forgive myself while forgiving my mother. Instead of scolding her, I gave her a kiss and told her how much I loved her.

LOVE DOES NOT PUNISH

One time, when I received a copy of my son Michael's report card from his school, I was surprised by his low grades and decided to give him a call. I wished to express my love for him, and my acceptance.

He was not very happy to hear from me and asked why I had called. I told him that I simply wished to tell him that I loved him. Then he asked if I had received his report card. I told him that I had, and that I knew he would do better next time. I also told him that it was important for him to let go of the past. He asked me if that was really why I had called. I repeated that I called simply to tell him that I loved him.

"Well, my mom loves me, too," he said.

"Of course she does," I assured him.

"She loves me more than you do," he continued.

"I know that she loves you unconditionally, as I do," I stated, rather confused by his remark. "We both love you very much."

"No, my mom loves me a lot more than you do," he added. "I know that she does, because she was very upset about my grades. She even punished me by taking away my computer and television privileges. That's why I know she loves me more than you do."

Still confused by his perception, I decided to let it go. I again told him that I loved him, and said goodnight.

I went to my meditation table to meditate, and my guide came up quickly. I asked him how my son could believe that I didn't love him because I didn't wish to punish him or make him feel guilty about his grades. My love for my son has always been unconditional.

My guide explained to me that Michael's belief system, like that of so many people on this planet, associated love with punishment. He said, "When they have done something that they or others judge to be incorrect or improper, they feel guilty. To relieve their guilt, they must be punished. In their eyes, the one who punishes them is the one who loves them."

He continued, "Many of you feel the same way about God. You feel abandoned or believe that He doesn't love you, because He doesn't punish you when you have done something that you feel guilty about. Because you grew up believing in 'the wrath of God,' you have an image of your Father as vengeful, angry and judgmental—but your Father is none of these things. He is like the sun; He shines light everywhere. His only desire is to shine the light of unconditional love and joy, which He is. He sees you as He created you: loving, joyful and magnificent. Anger, judgment and vengeance are darkness, and all darkness comes from Ego."

This lesson was very powerful for me. I began to see that whenever I had judged myself as not good enough—unworthy, undeserving and guilty—I had created the need within me to be punished. Since my Father wouldn't punish me, I had attracted other Egos that would contribute to me by punishing me and making me suffer. By resolving my guilt through punishment, my Ego had been justified and I could continue to do the same thing, over and over.

The truth is that our Father is love, joy, peace and happiness. He loves us unconditionally and He does not punish us. Only we can bring forth the punishment that we feel we deserve.

The next day when I picked my son up from school, I told him that I wished to share the powerful miracle that had come as a result of our conversation the night before. He was very open, and he listened carefully. When I was finished, he hugged me and said that it was true: whenever he had done something that he thought was wrong, he had waited to be punished, believing that punishment was a form of love and caring.

However, after hearing my powerful miracle, he could see how I had been unwilling to contribute to his guilt. Realizing this, he now understood that by not judging him, I was extending unconditional love and acceptance.

The more I share my miracles with my son, the more wonderful and holy our relationship becomes. Since I do not judge him as being too young or incapable of receiving the knowledge, he is also given the opportunity to grow from the lessons I am learning.

Every day I thank God for the blessings that come from communicating openly and honestly with other human beings.

SEEING THROUGH THE EYES
OF LOVE

In late 1998, on one of my trips to visit my mother and sister in Australia, an incredible miracle happened. I was at the airport waiting to board my Qantas flight when I noticed an old woman sitting across from me. She reminded me of the witch in *Snow White.* She had beady eyes, a long chin, and a very large nose with a wart on the end. Her hair looked dirty and stringy, and she seemed to be scowling.

When I became aware of how strong my judgment was about her, I felt uncomfortable and was in turmoil over it—until I remembered that how I see anyone or anything is only up to me. I am always able to control how I perceive things, simply by choosing to see them differently.

I decided that a shift in perception was needed, to bring me back to peace. I closed my eyes and began to imagine that the woman was my mother, who has unconditional love for me. I thought about my childhood, and how my mother had always hugged and kissed me, and comforted me when I was hurt.

As I continued to remember my mother, I began to feel a deep love and appreciation for the woman sitting across from me.

When I opened my eyes, I was surprised to see how different the woman looked. Her eyes were bright and sparkling. Her face had a glow about it and a huge smile that I had not seen before.

Noticing that I was looking at her, she waved at me to come and sit next to her. "I have brought some home cooking with me," she whispered. "Come sit over here and we can enjoy the food together." Immediately, I was filled with overwhelming love. I literally wanted to hug and kiss her.

For the next hour we ate, told jokes, and laughed. In my eyes, she had become one of the most beautiful women I had ever met. A deep sadness came over me as she left to board the plane at the gate next to mine.

That lovely woman brought me a powerful miracle. She showed me how quickly my perception can change, once I am willing to let go of judgment and bring forth unconditional love. As I had allowed myself to see who she truly was—a perfect child of God—her beautiful self had been able to shine through. Through this, I had found my way home to peace. I never saw the woman again, but I will never forget her smiling face and loving heart.

LETTING GO OF WHAT I WANT

One day, when my son Michael was eleven years old, he invited a couple of his friends over. We drove to their homes to pick them up and they sat in the back seat, while Michael sat in front with me.

Over the past few years, I had been holding Michael's hand whenever he was in the car with me; he enjoyed the unconditional love and warmth that we had for each other as much as I did. This time, however, when I held out my hand to take his, his response was different. Trying not to be noticed by his friends, he gently shook his head and very quietly said, "No."

I really wanted to hold his hand, so I opened my hand to him one more time and winked at him. Again, he shook his head, looking uncomfortable about the situation. "No," he insisted.

I let go of trying to persuade him. I gave up control of what I wanted and said to myself, "Let it be as it is." Michael and his friends were around eleven years old—the age when they do not wish to be seen as dependent upon their parents—so I felt that it was quite all right for me just to sit there and drive.

When we were about halfway home, one of Michael's friends asked me, "Mr. Anjomi, were you really Mr. Universe in 1993 and 1994?" "Yes," I replied.

"I would be very happy to have a father with the title of Mr. Universe," he said. Then he turned to Michael and said, "You are so lucky to have a father who is so nice to you, and who was Mr. Universe!"

Suddenly, Michael put his hand out and snapped his fingers, saying, "Daddy. Hand, hand." I put out my hand and he held it very, very tightly. He explained to his friends how much we love each other, and how much he appreciated me. He also told them that we hold hands as we ride in the car because we are so close and have such a good relationship. Both of the boys thought it was "awesome."

The most important lesson for me that day was about giving up control and not insisting that Michael hold my hand. I just allowed it to happen by itself. Whenever I put out my thought of what I want, and then let it go—instead of using my ego to persuade someone to do what I want him or her to do— whatever is good for me and the situation will happen, automatically and effortlessly. It will also bring a healing to the relationship. I felt good about that day. I had a wonderful time with the boys, and enjoyed myself completely.

THE LOVE OF GOD

A Course in Miracles says that if you think of a person you love most in this world and multiply the love you feel by a hundred times and then multiply *that* love by a thousand times, you will get only a glimpse of how much God loves you.

Wishing to experience this and to understand the magnitude of God's love, I meditated and brought forth my love for my son Michael. I multiplied my unconditional love for him by two, and then multiplied that love by three, and continued on. By the time I got to six, I could not multiply my love any higher; it was so strong and of such high quality that I desired to see my son and be with him every moment of the day.

From this experience of multiplying my love for my son, I realized that I could not even begin to comprehend the magnitude of God's love for me. Knowing this, I felt so safe and so loved in His hands that I was in total ecstasy and joy.

THE PATH OF LIFE

In 1990, after I had been studying *A Course in Miracles* for over a year, I entered a six-month period of heavy meditation and growth. During that time, I was not involved in a relationship.

Then one morning, after finishing my workout, I told my guide that it was about time for me to start dating someone. As I was leaving the gym, I noticed two women entering. We had never met, but I greeted them and chatted for a few minutes. At the end of the conversation, one of the women gave me her telephone number.

I called her later, and we went to dinner. As we got to know each other, I realized how compatible we were. The relationship began effortlessly, and it continued that way for over three years. During that time, we both experienced many miracles.

However, the relationship changed as time went on. Where we had previously enjoyed a very powerful, loving experience, we were now critical of one another. Just as she became jealous of my time with my son, I became aggravated by her time on the telephone while she was with me. We no longer enjoyed being in the present together. Within two months we broke up twice and then got back together, but we were still critical of one another.

After our third and final breakup, my greatest miracle occurred. A friend of mine who owned a nightclub suggested that I come to work there for a few hours on weekend nights. One Friday evening, my former girlfriend came into the club with several of her friends. I welcomed them and hugged her.

During the evening, she was joined by a man. They sat very close to where I was working and soon the two of them began to hold hands and kiss. I experienced great turmoil when I saw her with someone else, and to ease my discomfort, I moved to another area of the club.

After a couple of hours, I noticed that her friends were preparing to leave. When I asked them where she had gone, they said she had left with the man. I was confused and in pain. That Friday, I had one of my rare sleepless nights.

When I went to my meditation pyramid, I asked my guide for a way to peace. He told me to imagine myself on life's path, content and peaceful, until I came to a body of water. To cross the water, I needed a boat—in this case, *she* was the boat.

It had taken her over three years to carry me to the other side. During this effortless voyage, there was tremendous growth and there were many miracles. However, when we reached our destination, our journey together was over. After landing, I was supposed to continue on my path.

Then he asked me, "But did you do that? No." He continued by explaining that when I landed, I remembered how much fun my boat voyage had been, so I got back on the boat. But once aboard, I realized that we were not going anywhere. Again, I disembarked. This pattern repeated itself until I finally decided to continue along my path on land—but I did so by walking backwards and gazing at the boat. I kept looking to see who else got on, how she treated that person, and how that person treated her.

My guide concluded by saying, "Bijan, you cannot see what is in front of you by walking backwards." I was filled with peace.

The next night, my former girlfriend returned to the club and met the man there. As they passed by me to leave, she pulled her hand out of his. Seeing this, I introduced myself to the man, and then I hugged her. "She is a wonderful woman," I said to the man. Instead of having animosity or anger, I felt great love and appreciation toward my former girlfriend for the journey that we had taken together.

UNFORTUNATE CIRCUMSTANCES —OR GIFTS?

Often you may find that your Ego rises up, shouting and screaming over what seem to be unfortunate circumstances. Though at first you may not recognize the circumstances as gifts, it is best simply to accept them and know that ultimately you will see that they were.

For example, when you have an appointment or a date that does not show up, simply accept this as a gift from God, knowing that the appointment or date would not have been in your best interest. If you get fired from your job, accept it, and know that you were fired because there is a better job waiting for you. If something is not manifesting as you thought it would, understand that it is all perfect.

The simple truth is to trust God. Flow with the Universe. Know that absolutely everything is happening for your growth, and everything is a gift for you.

HEALING MY PERCEPTIONS

Over the years, I have healed my perception of hundreds of people in the gym. But the one who stands out the most is a man named Jack; he was unfriendly to everyone.

The first time I saw him, I walked up, extended my hand and said, "Good morning, my name is Bijan."

He gave me a cold look and very calmly said, "I know." Then he walked away.

Immediately, my Ego stepped in and tried to convince me that I was wasting my time. I refused to listen. Every morning, I would say "Hi," and Jack would ignore me. After about four months of persistence, he finally acknowledged me quietly by nodding his head. I knew that I had made progress, and from that point on, every time I said "Good morning," he would nod his head.

One day, I walked up to him, put my hand out and said, "Good morning, my name is Bijan."

He shook my hand and replied, "My name is Jack." He explained that he was somewhat shy, and did not like to talk to people in the gym.

I acknowledged that, thanked him and walked away.

About two years later, while I was talking to some friends at the gym, Jack walked in. The minute he saw me, a big smile lit up his face. "Good morning, Bijan!" he said.

My friends were quite surprised. They admitted to me that this was the first time they had ever seen him act that friendly toward anyone.

I was very pleased. Once again, I was reminded of how much I can heal my perception and grow when I am vigilant for the light, and not for Ego.

DECISION-MAKING IN THE PRESENT

I find that in making any decision, the information I most often wish to use comes from the past—from my ego. But to make the decision which will bring me peace, I must forget the past and decide without those old judgments.

At times this is very hard for me to do; sometimes I panic and wish to rely on information from the past. Yet, whenever I stay in the present and make my decision from that moment, asking God for guidance, the result is always great—it is even magnificent!

LOOKING BEYOND JUDGMENT

When I started healing my mind about people in the gym, I began by greeting anyone I had any kind of judgment toward. One of the most interesting experiences happened with a man who was tall, very big, incredibly masculine, and covered with tattoos. With his baseball cap turned backwards, he looked to me like a gang member who just got out of prison and was ready to hurt someone.

I thought to myself, "Oh, no! Now I have to greet him and heal my mind about *this* judgment!"

The man walked over to the heavyweight part of the gym and started to set up the bench press machine with free weights. He had several of the weights on each side—more than I had ever seen anyone else use. As I walked closer to him, he started to work out, making loud groaning and moaning noises that sounded very dangerous and scary.

I told myself, "Well, I can handle this some other time….when it's more appropriate."

But a voice said, "You have given your word to clear any judgment, and this is a judgment."

I took another step closer, but recalled that serious bodybuilders do not appreciate people bothering them while they are working out. Again, I said to myself, "No problem. I can see him when he is finished—tomorrow or some other day."

The voice said, "You have given your word, so keep your word."

With hesitation and an uncomfortable feeling, I slowly walked over to the man as he completed his set. I extended my hand and said, "Hello, my name is Bijan." I did not know what kind of reaction to expect from him, since he definitely did not look happy or friendly.

To my complete surprise, he put his hand out and shook mine warmly. "My name is Dan," he said.

As we started talking, I told him that he looked very strong and that he must have been working out for a long time. He said that he had been in several competitions, but only placed second, third, or fifth— never first. I told him this did not have anything to do with his size, how defined he was, or how he looked; it was all about *allowing* himself to receive the First Place trophy.

He seemed very interested in what I had to say, and invited me to sit down. This is not something bodybuilders do in the middle of a workout. We ended up having a warm conversation for almost thirty minutes. He was pleasant and very respectful.

When we finished and I went on my way, I had total love for this man and felt that he was one of the nicest people I had ever met. I laughed at myself, relieved to see how my perception changes whenever I am willing to look beyond my judgment.

About four days later, I saw Dan again. He had the same frown on his face as he did before, except this time he was also wearing dark glasses. My workout partner said, "Oh no…look at *that* guy!"

When Dan saw me, he took off his glasses and waved, but by the time I waved back, he already had his glasses back on, and the same frown was on his face again. No matter what my friend thought, I knew that under Dan's frown was a gentle and warm man, and I felt a deep love for him.

A PROBLEM WITH MEN

At one point in my life, I realized that I got along better with women than with men. After much deep thought and meditation, I found that there was a very easy way to correct this situation. Knowing that I truly loved myself, my father and my son, all that I had to do was to see *myself* in any man of my age, see *my father* in anyone older than I, and see *my son* in anyone younger.

Once I was able to see men this way, the problem was miraculously resolved. From that moment on, I no longer had a problem with men.

OUR FUNCTION

I had been studying *A Course in Miracles* religiously every day for several years, and once in a while I found myself asking myself the same question: "Why don't I feel the presence of God inside of me at every moment? Deep down, I know that I am always with Him and I know that He and I are communicating continuously."

Then I remembered that the course says that only a very small fraction of who we are is caught up in this dream of separation, and in this confusion and darkness, we have created the world. Wishing for more clarity, I decided to ask my guide, "Why am I more in touch with this thought of separation, which is so small, than with the much larger part of me that is connected to the Father?"

My guide answered with this example: "When you have a sore thumb, all of your attention goes to your thumb. You literally become your thumb. Your life with your Father's unconditional love is so effortless that it does not demand any attention. However, all of the healing and forgiveness has to be applied in this life to lighting up the darkness, or—in this example—healing your sore thumb. We always apply healing to where it is needed most."

He continued, saying, "The guilt that you have in your mind is only a small part of a huge deposit which lies in your subconscious. To heal your guilt, you must bring it up, piece by piece. You do this by projecting it onto someone else, so that you can see it in yourself. As you forgive and heal the person you projected your guilt onto, you forgive and heal yourself as well."

My guide had given me clarity about our function in this world. Our function is simply to heal ourselves and others, and nothing else. Everything in our lives—our relationships, our jobs, our dreams as we sleep, and our interactions with others—is a stepping-stone and an opportunity for healing ourselves and others.

WHERE WE DO GOD'S WORK

From the time I was a young boy of nine or ten years old, I had admired my older brother Michael's body. He was a devoted bodybuilder and used to pose for me. I began to train at the gym when I was about thirteen, and working out has continued to be a part of my daily life since then. Over the years, many studies have outlined the benefits of working out, describing the chemicals that are released in the process—but all I knew when I began was that I felt good. Working out was as natural to me as eating and sleeping.

After years of lifting weights, I yearned for the time when I could participate in some significant bodybuilding competitions. However, I was aware that I would need to use steroids to achieve the muscle mass necessary to compete successfully. Since I was definitely not interested in using drugs to alter my body, I just let it go.

Shortly after that, in January of 1993, I learned of several natural contests where all participants are screened by blood tests, urinalysis and/or lie detector tests. In February of 1993, I entered and won the Nevada competition; in April, I won for California; in June, I won for the United States, and in December, I captured the big one: Mr. Universe, Natural Division. Was body building my life? Most certainly not. The role of bodybuilding became very clear to me one evening during a seminar of *A Course in Miracles*.

One of the other students challenged my suggestion that we should move beyond the body to seek the love and light within ourselves. He demanded to know how I could say that, when I was obviously very involved in building my *own* body. I was stunned; I had never thought of myself in that way.

My response was spontaneous, and to this day reflects my honest feelings about my body, working out, and the gym. I explained that the gym offered me an abundance of miracles. On a daily basis, I was presented with many opportunities to practice the principles of *A Course in Miracles*. In fact, several of my friends from the gym had joined me at the seminar on Monday nights.

Even my titles facilitated growth in the gym; because of them, people approached me and inquired about fitness and training. This often opened the door for my functions of healing, loving and forgiving. Who are we to question where God guides us to do His work?

ON THE DEATH OF A LOVED ONE

I have always been extremely close to my mother. She and I have a connection that I have not shared with anyone else. While she was alive, I appreciated her counsel as much as her wit, and I visited her in Australia every year. Above all others, she marked my spiritual growth as I studied *A Course in Miracles*.

In the fall of 1992, my mother came to the United States for a visit. While here, she decided to travel to Calgary, Canada to see an old friend. My plan was that she would return and spend a few weeks with me in Las Vegas.

In November, I received a very somber telephone call from my brother John. He told me that Mother had suffered a heart attack. I was not distressed; instead, I treated it lightly. Perhaps even then I knew it was all perfect.

My brother continued, "No, Bijan—it is really serious. She is in a coma." He asked me to meet him in Canada.

When I arrived at the hospital, four hours after John, I walked into a room where a body lay. It was hooked up to tubes and machines. I recognized the body as my mother's, but she was definitely not occupying it. The doctor explained to us that we could request that the machines be disconnected. However, without our request, she would have to remain on them for several more days. I advised the doctor that we would let him know.

I told John that Mother was no longer in her body. He looked puzzled. I said that she would want us to have some fun and enjoy the city, since we would not be back here again. He looked bewildered and asked if I were sure of this. I asked him if it were not what Mom would want us to do. He agreed that it was.

Then I spoke to our mother. I told her that we wanted her to come back if she could—but if she could not, I wanted her to send us a sign to let her go.

As we left the hospital, John asked again if I were sure. "Let's go," I said. "Mom is not here." We went downtown and enjoyed ourselves as best we could.

The next day we returned to the hospital. Mother was in the same condition—the nurses said that nothing had changed. I asked if something had happened during the night, but each nurse said that nothing had. John looked at me and said, "Maybe she didn't hear you," but I knew that she had.

We waited for the doctor. His report was the same as those of the nurses. Mother's condition had not changed.

Again, I asked if something had occurred. The doctor asked me how I knew, and then went on to explain that, without apparent cause, all of the machines had stopped in the night.

We had our answer. John and I decided to call our sister Terry before instructing the doctor to disconnect the life support. Terry told us to do whatever we felt was best.

After we spoke to the doctor, we went to a mortuary to make the arrangements. Our options included cremation, burial in Canada, or shipping her somewhere else for burial.

John and I were inclined toward cremation. As we were discussing our decision, I became aware that Mother wanted to be buried next to our late brother Michael and his two sons. When I talked about this with John, he immediately agreed.

We told the mortician of our decision. He offered to check the availability of flights on which her body could be shipped, but when he returned a few minutes later, the news was not good. There were no flights available to San Jose, California for the next five days.

Since John and I were leaving that evening, we were uncomfortable with her body remaining in Canada. As we were packing in the hotel room, the telephone rang. It was the mortician. He told us, with amazement, that he had received notification from the airlines that there was cargo space available that evening. To our surprise, it was on John's flight.

When John contacted the San Jose cemetery to make the arrangements for Mother, he was told that the plot next to Michael's was not available, and the closest one was across the way. Disappointed, we decided to take it.

On the day that Mother was to be buried, John received a telephone call from the funeral director, informing him that the person who owned the grave next to Michael's had defaulted. The site next to my brother was now available.

From the morning after my mother left her body, she has joined me in my regular meditations. Each day, her presence continues to give me guidance and love.

HEALING

We are all capable of healing ourselves and others, as long as we let go of fear, let go of control, and understand that we are not the ones who are doing the healing. Natural healing is done by the Universe through us, as we recognize our oneness with the person being healed. In this joining, both parties benefit.

Although I did not plan to become a healer, I had read in *A Course in Miracles* that it is natural for us to heal; it is our function in this world. I was working in a nightclub when I first started to do healing. I would relieve the headaches of friends who suffered from the loud noise, and on many occasions, the bartender would refer people to me when they requested aspirin. Although the process was not something that I controlled, I soon became sensitive to when the healing was complete, because a tremendous sense of peace would wash over me. However, I could only heal people if they truly desired to be healed.

After several months of experience in healing, I met a trainer at the gym. His knee was wrapped and he was obviously in a lot of pain. I asked about his injury, and he told me the extent of the problem in medical terms that I did not understand. I asked if he desired to be healed. "Of course I do," he replied.

He was scheduled for surgery in two days. We held hands and I felt myself enter his body. While I was there, I vaguely recognized his pain. I asked the Father to heal me.

Once back in my own body, I was overcome with a tremendous sense of peace. As we dropped our hands, he remarked that his pain had subsided and that he could now move around freely, without discomfort. When he went to see the doctor for his preoperative visit, he was advised that surgery was no longer necessary.

A few weeks later, a woman who had a neck injury came to see me at the gym; the trainer had sent her. She was facing a difficult back surgery and was in great pain. I asked if she desired to be healed. When she said that she did, we went to a corner of the gym and joined hands. I felt myself enter her body, and actually felt my own neck being pulled to one side; I was now sharing her pain. Once again, I asked the Father to heal me. When the tremendous peace overcame me, we separated.

She was amazed that her pain was gone. Her first question was, "Do I still have to have the surgery?" I advised her to consult her doctor. Her second question was the one most often asked of me; "What did you do?" To this day, I really do not know how the healing occurs—I simply know that it is not of me.

GUIDED BY SPIRIT

As most of us were growing up, we were taught the importance of being in control. We learned to believe that the more control we have over our life and the lives of others, the happier we will be. This kind of control is in the realm of Ego, and Ego will always guide you into turmoil. In truth, the more you surrender control to Spirit—taking the control away from Ego—the more you will be guided in the right direction, which is toward peace.

Imagine jumping into a river while wearing a life jacket. As you float downstream and find yourself drawing nearer and nearer to some large rocks, you can choose to be guided by Ego or by Spirit. If you give control to Ego, it will tell you to react in fear and to struggle against the current's natural flow. You will create such turmoil by trying to swim against the current to avoid flowing toward the rocks, that you will finally wear yourself out.

However, if you surrender control to Spirit, you will know that when you *let go* of Ego (fear) the current will carry you along effortlessly. As you float peacefully in the water—becoming one with it instead of resisting it—the current's natural flow will guide you. When you simply give up control, with little intention of going anywhere other than where the current leads, you will be carried where you are supposed to go and where it is best for you.

TO KNOW WHAT YOU WANT, LOOK AT WHAT YOU HAVE

Whenever you are unhappy about an experience in your life, it is important to remember that on some level you have *asked* for the experience and have *accepted* it for yourself. In order to change what you receive in your life, it is necessary for you first to *release* what you do not wish to have, and then to *ask* for what you *truly desire.* The Universe will always fulfill your wishes to the degree that you keep your word in your life. Remember to keep your word.

Refer back to the first three readings:
About Ego (p. 53)
Keeping Your Word (p. 55)
You Always Get What You Want (p. 57)

GLOSSARY

*Be
vigilant
for the light.*

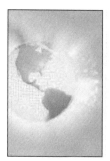

Effortless Prosperity is about *being* in the present. In the present moment, we are totally provided for as precious children of God. We need not *do* anything that comes from Ego in order to be effortlessly prosperous; miracles simply show up constantly and effortlessly. We become the creators of our universe, manifesting everything we ask for. To have effortless prosperity is to be in total peace.

Ego is the small part of the mind that we created out of fear. Ego loves darkness and turmoil, and it loves *stories* about darkness and turmoil. It lives in the *guilt* of the past and the *fear* of the future. Ego blocks and denies our ability to bring forth our inheritance from our Creator; through its denial of our inner goodness, it undermines our attempts to grow to higher levels. Ego speaks to us in the languages of criticism, judgment, insecurity, scarcity, separation, sacrifice and fear. When we listen to Ego, turmoil is always the result.

Extension is the way in which God creates. He extended Himself and created us. When we share our love, we are extending as God does.

Function is our mission while we are here on Earth. Our function is to heal ourselves and others through love and forgiveness.

Healing is our function. It is what occurs when our minds join with the minds of our sisters and brothers, to experience wholeness. When we join in healing, we release our feelings of guilt and sin and replace them with joy and peace.

Joy is the door we walk through, to reach peace.

Judgment is our distorted opinion. It is our Ego's mistaken belief that we have all of the facts necessary to evaluate and discern. When we judge others, we are really judging ourselves.

Light (spiritual light) is anything which brings joy, peace, love, healing, and deeper spirituality. It is the Divine Presence in each of us. Light is the illumination of our higher self.

Miracle is a shift in perception. It is the natural state of things when the flow of life is unobstructed. Miracles occur when, through the help of Spirit, we offer forgiveness and love instead of judgment and attack, to a sister or brother. Miracles create healing, which releases us from guilt, fear and anger. Miracles are not sized.

Peace is a sense of well-being and calmness that allows light to flow through us, and allows miracles to be recognized more easily. It occurs when we are in the present moment and are not living in the past or future. Peace is our ultimate goal. We acquire it through healing, by forgiving and loving.

Perception is our interpretation of the world we live in. It is distorted by Ego and is always changing, because it is based on the Ego's judgments. *See also Shift in perception.*

Projection is the process by which we get rid of our guilt, fear and anger by thrusting them onto someone or something else. What we see outside of ourselves is simply a reflection of what we see inside of ourselves.

Prosperity is not simply about having financial abundance; it is about having excellent health and joyful relationships, too. Without all of these things, we cannot be in peace. When we are in peace, we have prosperity in *every* area of our lives.

Shift in perception is when we choose to see an experience differently. Instead of listening to our Ego, which brings up fear and guilt, we listen to Holy Spirit and extend the love of God, which brings us peace. A shift in perception is a miracle.

Spirit is often referred to as Holy Spirit. Spirit speaks to us in the languages of love, truth, joy and faith; it is our oneness with God. When we follow Spirit's guidance, we experience joy, peace, abundance and growth.

Story always talks about history—about the *past*. A story is never about the present moment. Often, Ego will add drama and exaggeration to a story, for more effect. When a story is used to preface a miracle, it brings turmoil to the speaker and to the listener.

Vigilant for the light means that we constantly monitor our thoughts and monitor what we see, hear and say. Remember that we are not here to monitor others; we are here to be vigilant for the light in *ourselves* and in our *interactions* with others. Vigilance requires that we consciously choose only thoughts, conversations, activities and relationships that will keep us in the light. Vigilant is about being, not about *doing*. It is about being *steadfast*.

MIRACLE
JOURNAL

Miracles are like wild pigeons.
the more you feed them,
the more they show up
and bring their friends.

Notice your miracles!

DAY 1 ~ LESSON 1
I Watch What I Say

_____

_____

_____

_____

_____

_____

_____

_____

_____

_____

_____

_____

_____

_____

_____

_____

_____

_____

_____

_____

Affirmation: I speak only for peace.
Remember to keep your word today.

_____

_____

_____

_____

_____

_____

_____

_____

_____

_____

_____

_____

_____

_____

_____

_____

_____

_____

_____

_____

Affirmation: I listen only for peace.
Remember to keep your word today.

_____

_____

_____

_____

_____

_____

_____

_____

_____

_____

_____

_____

_____

_____

_____

_____

_____

_____

_____

Affirmation: I see peace everywhere.
Remember to keep your word today.

I Do Not Know the Real Meaning of What I See

_____

_____

_____

_____

_____

_____

_____

_____

_____

_____

_____

_____

_____

_____

_____

_____

_____

_____

_____

Affirmation: I am surrounded by peace.

Remember to keep your word today.

I Am Willing To See the Light

_____

_____

_____

_____

_____

_____

_____

_____

_____

_____

_____

_____

_____

_____

_____

_____

_____

Affirmation: I know only peace inside.
Remember to keep your word today.

Affirmation: I am vigilant for peace.
Remember to keep your word today.

I Am Very Prosperous

Affirmation: I am so peaceful.
Remember to keep your word today.

Everyone Wishes To Contribute To Me

Affirmation: I see peace in everyone's actions.

Remember to keep your word today.

I Deserve Prosperity

_____

_____

_____

_____

_____

_____

_____

_____

_____

_____

_____

_____

_____

_____

_____

_____

_____

_____

Affirmation: My planet Earth deserves peace.
Remember to keep your word today.

I Am Open To Receive All of God's Gifts

_____

_____

_____

_____

_____

_____

_____

_____

_____

_____

_____

_____

_____

_____

_____

_____

_____

_____

_____

_____

_____

Affirmation: I see world peace.
Remember to keep your word today.

I Give As I Receive

_____

_____

_____

_____

_____

_____

_____

_____

_____

_____

_____

_____

_____

_____

_____

_____

_____

_____

Affirmation: I wish peace for everyone.
Remember to keep your word today.

I Release All Fear

_____

_____

_____

_____

_____

_____

_____

_____

_____

_____

_____

_____

_____

_____

_____

_____

_____

_____

_____

_____

_____

_____

Affirmation: I embrace only peace.
Remember to keep your word today.

I Open My Mind to Peace

_____

_____

_____

_____

_____

_____

_____

_____

_____

_____

_____

_____

_____

_____

_____

_____

_____

_____

Affirmation: I open my life to peace.

Remember to keep your word today.

I Recognize My Own Best Interest

Affirmation: Peace is all I desire.

Remember to keep your word today.

I Am Patient

_____

_____

_____

_____

_____

_____

_____

_____

_____

_____

_____

_____

_____

_____

_____

_____

_____

_____

Affirmation: Peace is forever.
Remember to keep your word today.

I Pause Before I React

_____

_____

_____

_____

_____

_____

_____

_____

_____

_____

_____

_____

_____

_____

_____

_____

_____

_____

_____

Affirmation: I love peace.
Remember to keep your word today.

I Am Open To Receive Miracles

_____

_____

_____

_____

_____

_____

_____

_____

_____

_____

_____

_____

_____

_____

_____

_____

_____

_____

_____

Affirmation: I see everyone peaceful.
Remember to keep your word today.

DAY 18 ~ LESSON 18
I Choose Only Peace

_____

_____

_____

_____

_____

_____

_____

_____

_____

_____

_____

_____

_____

_____

_____

_____

_____

_____

_____

Affirmation: I love my peace.
Remember to keep your word today.

I Am Loving and Lovable

_____

_____

_____

_____

_____

_____

_____

_____

_____

_____

_____

_____

_____

_____

_____

_____

_____

_____

_____

Affirmation: God shines peace on me.
Remember to keep your word today.

Only Love Exists; Fear Is an Illusion

_____

_____

_____

_____

_____

_____

_____

_____

_____

_____

_____

_____

_____

_____

_____

_____

_____

_____

_____

Affirmation: Peace is within me.
Remember to keep your word today.

God Loves Me Unconditionally

_____

_____

_____

_____

_____

_____

_____

_____

_____

_____

_____

_____

_____

_____

_____

_____

_____

_____

Affirmation: I feel God's peace now.
Remember to keep your word today.

God Loves Me More Than I Love Myself

_____

_____

_____

_____

_____

_____

_____

_____

_____

_____

_____

_____

_____

_____

_____

_____

_____

_____

_____

_____

Affirmation: God's peace and mine are one.

Remember to keep your word today.

I Trust God

_____

_____

_____

_____

_____

_____

_____

_____

_____

_____

_____

_____

_____

_____

_____

_____

_____

_____

Affirmation: I trust peace.

Remember to keep your word today.

God Is Great, and So Am I

_____

_____

_____

_____

_____

_____

_____

_____

_____

_____

_____

_____

_____

_____

_____

_____

_____

_____

_____

_____

Affirmation: Peace is great.
Remember to keep your word today.

I Let Go and Let God

_____

_____

_____

_____

_____

_____

_____

_____

_____

_____

_____

_____

_____

_____

_____

_____

_____

_____

Affirmation: I shine peace.
Remember to keep your word today.

I Am Blessed As a Child of God

_____

_____

_____

_____

_____

_____

_____

_____

_____

_____

_____

_____

_____

_____

_____

_____

_____

_____

_____

_____

_____

Affirmation: I have the peace of God.
Remember to keep your word today.

Today Belongs to God; It Is My Gift to Him

_____

_____

_____

_____

_____

_____

_____

_____

_____

_____

_____

_____

_____

_____

_____

_____

_____

_____

_____

_____

Affirmation: I am one with peace.
Remember to keep your word today.

DAY 28 ~ LESSON 28
I See Only God in All of My Affairs

Affirmation: Peace is everywhere.
Remember to keep your word today.

_____

_____

_____

_____

_____

_____

_____

_____

_____

_____

_____

_____

_____

_____

_____

_____

_____

Affirmation: Thank you, peaceful Earth.
Remember to keep your word today.

Affirmation: I am peace.

Remember to keep your word today.

EPILOGUE

*This is not an end to your experience,
but rather the beginning of your growth.*

*Be open to the possibilities, and remember—
who you **really** are
has nothing to do
with what you think of yourself,
but
everything that happens outside of you
is a direct result of what you think of yourself.*

ABOUT BIJAN

Bijan Anjomi is a man who is making a difference. Author, speaker, founder of Effortless Prosperity Seminars, success coach and a visionary for world peace, he lectures internationally in the fields of health, spirituality and spontaneous living.

Born in Persia and raised as a student of the Baha'i, Judaic and Muslim faiths, Bijan came to the United States when he was 19 years old. In the years that followed, his natural curiosity led him along many paths. To name a few, he owned a health club—worked as a bartender, maitre 'd and a bouncer in bars—attended college—became a commercial real estate agent—studied various forms of meditation—attained his certification as a clinical hypnotherapist—and captured the title of Mr. Universe, Natural Division for 1993 and 1994.

The evolution of Bijan-the-author began in the late 1980's, when he began studying, practicing, and finally teaching the principles set forth in *A Course in Miracles*. Over the next nine years, he noticed that his life was gradually changing for the better; by the mid-90's, his health was flawless, his relationships were joyful and harmonious, and all that he desired was being provided without effort. At this point, his higher consciousness—or guide, as Bijan refers to him—appeared, and asked him to write a book called *Absolutely Effortless Prosperity*. Bijan admits that he was, to put it mildly, not very receptive to the idea, as he had never found reading or writing to be a particularly joyful activity. Regardless, he finally agreed to write the book. The first edition of *Absolutely Effortless Prosperity* was self-published in February of 1997 for a small group of people who were invited to be part of a thirty-day seminar. Within a month, the Las Vegas Effortless Prosperity Center opened, and study groups were meeting every two hours from morning 'til night, seven days a week. And then, through miracles and word-of-mouth, this simple book of thirty lessons was falling into the hands of people everywhere.

In the next two years, Bijan hosted his own radio show in Las Vegas, appeared on radio and TV talk shows in Los Angeles, San Francisco, Las Vegas and New York, and became a regular guest on WOR New York's nationally syndicated *Joey Reynolds Show*. He was further guided to bring forth books for children and teenagers, a book on health, and the next set of lessons for adults—all following the basic principles of *Absolutely Effortless Prosperity*.

Through the guidance of his higher consciousness, he has been directed to manifest his works for one purpose: world peace. The purpose of his books, tapes, seminars and workshops is to assist people in opening their hearts to joy and peace—experiencing and believing in it, and living in the reality of it.

To this end, Bijan continues reaching out to people worldwide, through speaking engagements, television, radio, personal coaching, and through his Web site. He has guided many students of his original classes to go forth as study group facilitators in prisons, shelters and dependency groups, and has watched the blossoming of the programs for children. As more and more employers are beginning to schedule meditation or "spirituality breaks" for their employees, he is also hearing news about study groups in the workplace. The light of Effortless Prosperity is steadily growing brighter and stronger, as people step forth to translate the writings into other languages: the Spanish edition of *Prosperidad Sin Esfuerzo* has been in Mexico since 1998, the Persian (Farsi) translation was introduced in early 2000, while French, Italian, Dutch, Chinese, Japanese and Polish translations are in process.

Bijan's vision is simple yet profound. The basic truth is these words he speaks, time and again: *"As more and more people begin to experience joyful, peaceful, abundant living, the barriers between countries, cultures and religious philosophies will simply melt away."*

CREATE A STUDY GROUP
Two or more people who are vigilant for the light
are much more powerful than hundreds of people
living in darkness.

A STUDY GROUP IS...
An Effortless Prosperity Study Group consists of two or more people who come together to grow in the light and share miracles. It is a thirty-day program that begins on the first day of the month and concludes on the thirtieth day, with a celebration.

- Each meeting begins with the joining of hands in a circle as one of the participants—or a facilitator—says a few words to bring the group together in spirit.
- This is followed by the reading of the day's lesson and assignment, or by listening to Bijan's tape for the day from the *Book I* or *Book II* companion tape set. The remainder of the meeting is filled with the sharing of miracles.
- Giving is receiving and receiving is giving—in many groups, a donation basket is passed around before the close of each meeting, and at the end of the month, the groups use the money to create joy and make miracles happen through charitable acts.
- The meeting is brought to a close with a joining of hands, as a facilitator or one of the participants says a few words.

An Effortless Prosperity study group is a gathering place of joy, peace, light and love. It is not a therapy session, a 12-step program, or a religious meeting—it is simply a place to gather for the purpose of sharing miracles of the day. Because of this, study groups are adaptable to every imaginable environment—home, the workplace, the gym, church groups, senior centers, detention centers, hospitals—wherever there are people.

In a study group, there is no preaching or advising, nor is there networking or business talk; darkness is never shared, nor are long stories that often invite it. Sharing miracles is most important. The effect is so powerful that eventually those in the group will begin to share miracles with everyone they meet, and will begin to notice the light in everything they do. Miraculously, their lives will be transformed—they will see people differently; relationships will either become joyful or they will end for the best interest of all; they will feel healthy and happy for no particular reason, and will experience abundance in their lives.
Effortless Prosperity study groups all over the world follow these guidelines—and as every group focuses on the same lesson on the same day of the month, each of us aligns with the collective consciousness of

all our sisters and brothers in the light. There is tremendous power and effectiveness that comes forth when so many people around the world are doing the same lesson on the same day. The global and personal benefits of Effortless Prosperity multiply greatly.

FACILITATING...

Facilitating a study group is both fun and enlightening; it can be a source of great joy and inspiration in your life, and need not consume much of your time or energy. All that is required for starting your own group is the desire to be more open to joy and peace, and the desire to share joy and peace with others. When you simply create the space for people to join together, read the day's lesson, and share your own shifts in perception, you will open the other participants to becoming aware of the miracles in their own lives. It can be the one place where everyone leaves all problems outside the door and is enveloped in the light.

AS YOU CREATE A STUDY GROUP...

We'd love to hear about it! You can let us know by phone, fax, or mail, or drop us a line at groups@effortlessprosperity.com. Let us know your name, address, city and state, the time of day that you meet, and any other pertinent information about your group. We plan on posting a list of ongoing study groups worldwide.

AND SEND US YOUR MIRACLES!

Has your life changed since studying the *Effortless Prosperity* books? Do you have some miracles you would like to share with the world? Has your study group created some magnificent miracles in your community? We are in the process of assembling the first book of Effortless Prosperity miracles. If you would like to empower others by including your personal miracles and testimonials in this book, please send them to us, completing and signing the form in this catalog. If one of your miracles is selected to be included in the book, we'll send you an autographed copy in appreciation.

Special Note: Your personal miracles can only be considered if they are accompanied by a signed release. All submissions will become the property of Effortless Prosperity, Inc. Thank you!

MIRACLE SHARE

Always remember Bijan's Law:
**Everything that CAN go right, WILL go right.
EXPECT MIRACLES!**

Visit us at www.effortless prosperity.com or,

In the space below and on the following page, please write down the growth you have experienced since you have been participating in Effortless Prosperity, and share some of your favorite miracles with us. Attach additional sheets if necessary. Effortless Prosperity reserves the right to abbreviate or modify your story for the purposes of publication.

_____

_____

_____

_____

_____

_____

_____

_____

_____

_____

(there is room to write more on the back of this page)

I am happy to give permission to Effortless Prosperity to share all or part of my testimonial and miracles with the world!

Print Full Name_____

Signature_____Date_____

Phone(_____)_____ Email _____

EFFORTLESS ORDER FORM

Qty	BOOKS	U.S.	Total
_____	Absolutely Effortless Prosperity, Book I	$15	_____
_____	Absolutely Effortless Prosperity, Book I, Chinese	$18	_____
_____	Absolutely Effortless Prosperity, Book I, Dutch	$18	_____
_____	Absolutely Effortless Prosperity, Book I, French	$18	_____
_____	Absolutely Effortless Prosperity, Book I, German	$18	_____
_____	Absolutely Effortless Prosperity, Book I, Italian	$18	_____
_____	Absolutely Effortless Prosperity, Book I, Japanese	$18	_____
_____	Absolutely Effortless Prosperity, Book I, Persian	$18	_____
_____	Absolutely Effortless Prosperity, Book I, Polish	$18	_____
_____	Absolutely Effortless Prosperity, Book I, Spanish	$18	_____
_____	Absolutely Effortless Prosperity, Book II	$15	_____
_____	The Common Sense of Effortless Health	$10	_____
_____	Common Sense Tips for Effortless Health	$18	_____
_____	Little Friends Of Nature, Book I, For Children Ages 2 to 7	$10	_____
_____	Little Friends Of Nature, Book II	$10	_____
_____	My Guiding Spirit, Book I, For Children Ages 8 to 12	$10	_____
_____	My Guiding Spirit, Book II	$10	_____
_____	Light From The Sky, Book I, For Teenagers 13 to 18	$10	_____
_____	Light From The Sky, Book II	$10	_____
_____	Effortless Laughter, 2002 Edition	$10	_____
_____	Miracles Happen!	$15	_____
_____	Bookmark, 30 Effortless Lessons	$1	_____

EFFORTLESS ORDER FORM

Qty	TAPES	U.S.	Total
_____	**Absolutely Effortless Prosperity, Book I** 16-Tape Set, Includes Meditation Tape	$75	_____
_____	**Absolutely Effortless Prosperity, Book II** 16-Tape Set, Includes Laughter Tape	$75	_____
_____	Attain Mastery	$10	_____
_____	Common Sense of Effortless Health	$10	_____
_____	Effortless Affirmations For Everyone	$10	_____
_____	Giving and Receiving	$10	_____
_____	Having an Effortless and Joyous Job	$10	_____
_____	Healing in the New Millennium	$10	_____
_____	How To Be Open to Receive, Volume I	$35	_____
_____	How To Be Open to Receive, Volume II	$35	_____
_____	Manifesting Consciously	$10	_____
_____	Meditation	$8	_____

Shipping and Handling Rates

Up to $50 - $5.00	$101 - $150 - $15.00	
$51 - $100 - $10.00	$151 - $240 - $20.00	

Subtotal _____

Shipping & Handling _____

NV residents add 7.25% sales tax _____

TOTAL _____

TO PLACE YOUR ORDER:

Credit Card Orders:	TOLL FREE 1-800-437-7750
On-line orders:	www.effortlessprosperity.com
Mail orders:	Real People Publishing Group
	6655 West Sahara, Suite B200
	Las Vegas, NV 89146-2832
Fax Orders:	702-222-1644

Prices subject to change without notice.
Please call or write for study group or volume discounts.

EFFORTLESS PAYMENT METHODS

☑ I have enclosed a check or money order payable to Real People Publishing Group

Please Charge My:

☑ VISA ☑ MasterCard ☑ Discover ☑ American Express

Number:___ ___ ___ ___-___ ___ ___ ___-___ ___ ___ ___-___ ___ ___ ___

Expiration date: _____/_____

Signature:_____

Billing Address (Exactly as shown on credit card)

Name: _____

Address: _____Apt./Unit:_____

City:_____ State:_____ Zip+ 4:_____ -_____

Day Phone: _____-_____Evening Phone: _____

Ship To:

Name: _____

Shipping Address: _____Apt./Unit:_____

City:_____ State:_____ Zip+ 4:_____ -_____

Day Phone: _____-_____Evening Phone: _____

Email Address: _____

Website Address: _____

☑ YES! I would like to be on your mailing list to receive updated product information and newsletters.

Please come visit us at:
www.effortlessprosperity.com

We have established a worldwide community
of people who come together
to share miracles.
We would love to hear of *your* miracles.

Also, learn of Bijan's live appearances and
other products to help further your growth.

Or if the web is not effortless for you;
call toll-free 1-800-437-7750
to find out more.

Love and Light,
Bijan

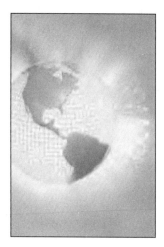

This book is going to help and support you by focusing your thoughts on peace and spirit. You must know that it is a world of belief systems, meaning whatever you think and believe, you experience.

By learning how to control your thoughts more and more, through the daily lessons that focus on peace, joy, love, and prosperity, you will soon notice that you will start to think differently about each situation and you will truly experience a more effortless life.